HOLD
ON
LET
GO

What people said about *Lifelines*, the prequel to *Hold On, Let Go*

'*A great guide full of clear, simple and useful wisdom on how to live and lovely reminders of what we too often forget.*'
Matt Haig
Bestselling author of *The Humans* and *How To Stop Time*

'*This book feels like balm to my weary heart. It's beautiful, wise, and, maybe most importantly, playful … The authors know how to meet people where they are.*'
Brené Brown
Research professor and author of the *New York Times*' #1 bestseller *Braving the Wilderness*

'*Lifelines is about those things in life we cannot see, that might change how we view the things we can. A book of faith for those wary of religion. Sacred text for the more earthy reader.*'
Bono

'*I really like this very fine book … Makes me think it will find a lot of readers and a lot of YES.*'
Richard Rohr
OFM, Franciscan, writer and speaker

'*Just gorgeous bite-sized pieces of love throughout. Beautiful work.*'
Ava DuVernay
Award-winning writer/director of *Selma*, *13th* and *A Wrinkle in Time*

'*A wonderfully rich collection of insightful, inspiring and humorous reflections.*'
Nick Park
Oscar-winning director and creator of *Wallace and Gromit*

MALCOLM DONEY · MARTIN WROE

HOLD
ON
LET
GO

HOW TO FIND YOUR LIFE

wild goose
publications

www.**iona**books.com

First published 2023 by
Wild Goose Publications
Suite 9, Fairfield
1048 Govan Road, Glasgow G51 4XS, Scotland
A division of Iona Community Trading CIC
Limited Company Reg. No. SC156678
www.ionabooks.com

ISBN 978-1-80432-304-5

Cover painting and book illustrations © Malcolm Doney
Cover design © Jeff Fisher

Overseas distribution
Australia: Willow Connection Pty Ltd, 1/13 Kell Mather Drive,
Lennox Head NSW 2478
New Zealand: Pleroma, Higginson Street, Otane 4170,
Central Hawkes Bay

Printed in the UK by Page Bros (Norwich) Ltd

INSIDE

HOLD ON, LET GO

Lovely and cruel. Simple and difficult. Extraordinary and quotidian.

Sometimes on the same day.

Life.

And the questions it asks that we carry around with us. Questions as old as our oldest ancestor and as fresh as that coffee brewing.

Why is there something rather than nothing?

What is this thing called love?

Why did she have to get sick?

How come music makes me cry?

We once looked for answers in churches or synagogues, in mosques or temples and over several thousand years those great households of religion claimed a monopoly on the answers.

But many of us stopped believing in them and stopped belonging to them.

We're fine sitting in the tranquillity of some ancient house of prayer, but please don't tell us what to believe.

We're shy of certainty, suspicious of authority, but still, those questions ...

Is there some hidden current to carry us through our days? The resonance of some distant melody. How the big moments – the birth of a child, say, or the death of a friend – may leave us wondering about how to live in the small moments.

If love is worth it.

How to forgive someone.

Why people pray.

What is a good life?

Some days we hold on.

Others we let go.

What nourishes us and makes us strong? What's worth keeping hold of? And what should we let go?

Take faith. Or leave it. For one person it's a reason for being. For another it's what they must shed to find themselves.

This small collection of field notes is less of a 'how to' book than a 'try this' book.

It's about keeping your feet on this sacred earth. And taking wing. At the same time.

Malcolm Doney, Martin Wroe, August 2023

GREET THE DAY

How many mornings will we get?

No one can tell.

The accident of birthplace has a say on the number of our days. But, roughly speaking, we might find the sun rising and peeking through our curtains about 26,000 times.

Most of those days we will never remember.

And a few we will never forget.

Nearly a century ago, the poet and children's author Eleanor Farjeon wrote 'Morning Has Broken', a hymn which captures a sense of gratitude for a new day. She imagined the first morning in Eden, with Adam and Eve taking in the birdsong, the dew on the grass, the breaking light. Much later the hymn became a pop hit for Cat Stevens, who continued to perform it under his new name, Yusuf Islam, after converting to Islam.

Whether we give God a name or whether we don't, giving thanks is a good way to start the day.

What might happen on any given day?

No one can tell.

Every day is a surprise.

All we can know for sure is that, as each new morning breaks, she is there again.

She is ours.

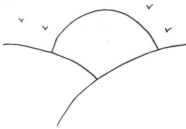

FIND THE GOLDEN HOUR

Photographers and filmmakers call it 'the golden hour'. That moment, just before the sun rises or sets, when the light is softer and warmer than at any other time in the day.

Emmanuel 'Chivo' Lubezki, the Oscar-winning cinematographer on *The Revenant*, insisted on shooting the film only in this short window. 'As they say, you know,' said the star of the movie Leonardo DiCaprio, 'that's when God speaks.'

The quality of light distinguishes these twilight moments early in the morning and late in the evening. They also form a buffer zone between night and day, between day and night. This borderland is more than meteorological or chronological; it has emotional, spiritual and artistic echoes too.

Anticipating daybreak or nightfall, we might feel trepidation or excitement. The daily cycle calls to mind a world of beginnings and endings: of natural ebb and flow, but also transitions in relationships, career, location; entrances and exits, birth and death.

In the morning twilight, on a good day, you may take a deep breath, and allow the imagination to send out its search parties – listening for signals, making connections. With that first cup of tea steaming in your hand, the day's prospects unfurl before you.

As the misty half-light grows more luminous, as those scurrying scouting parties of the wakening imagination report back, more often than not, you begin to see possibilities.

Just supposing ... what if ... here's a thought ...

The golden hour, when the light speaks to you.

Curtain

Through a gap
In the curtain
The light arrives
Eight minutes
Twenty seconds
Ninety-three million miles

From the sun
To my window,
I open my eyes,
All this way
To bring us a day
Better try and do it right.

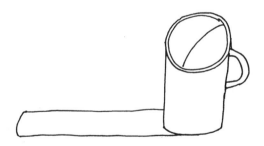

RECORD YOUR DAYS

We're all trying to get a better view of ourselves.

But with so much of ourselves to see, perspective is hard to come by.

One way to bring life into focus is in the simple act of setting pen to notepad, in keeping a regular journal.

From the messiest scribble to the patient entry, a diary freeze-frames who we are. Right now.

Writing down our day slows our racing thoughts, offering a brief chance to see them in some kind of perspective. To get a feel for the shape of this life. It helps us, says Joan Didion, 'remember what it was to be me: That is always the point.'

In *The Artist's Way*, written to help people harness their innate creativity, Julia Cameron popularised the notion of producing 'Morning Pages' as a path to clear-headedness. She recommends putting all your thoughts on the page for half an hour – including everything that's going wrong, the self-doubt, the criticism, the anxiety ... Once we get those muddy, maddening, confusing thoughts on the page, she says, we face our day with clearer eyes. We are more candid with ourselves, more centred, and more spiritually at ease.

Some mornings we will have no time; on others we will have nothing to say. But a journal entry doesn't have to be long or deep. It may be a simple sketch or list: music you're listening to; films you've seen; a novel that touched you.

Or as simple as a note of what someone said to you which you'd like to remember.

Other entries may dive deeper: about why a relationship has gone pear-shaped ... or whether you really could change career. Even entries which seem like a dump of inarticulate feelings can, later, glint with moments of clarity.

It can help to write by hand, not on screen, to set aside a notebook which you don't use for anything else – and to keep it private. You can be a more honest writer if you know you're the only reader.

A diary may only be cursory, a snapshot. But over time it can become an increasingly reliable witness to your life. As you re-read entries from months or years before, a journal can become a map of your days, warning you about blind alleys, and, in hilly terrain, encouraging you with a reminder of the view ahead.

Step out of the routine of daily obligations for a moment.

Take a look at your life in the round.

Record your days.

See who you are.

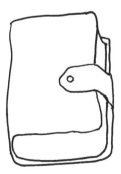

PRACTISE KINDNESS

'Practise random kindness and senseless acts of beauty.'

The phrase can be traced back to a note written on a placemat in a Californian restaurant thirty-odd years ago by Anne Herbert. She went on to write a book documenting acts of kindness and the idea became a cultural meme influencing films like *Evan Almighty*, in which God tells the hero Evan to change the world with one act of random kindness at a time.

But what if God was wrong?

Why leave kindness to chance?

Why not make kindness deliberate, planned and organised?

Any of us would do that if we understood the power of another phrase that has occupied the zeitgeist: 'Be kind, for everyone you meet is fighting a hard battle.'

What the nineteenth-century Scottish writer Ian Maclaren was asking of us, when he first coined this phrase, was what today we call 'empathy'. That's a quality we cannot underestimate, according to anthropologist Jane Goodall: 'Empathy is really important. Only when our clever brain and our human heart work together in harmony can we achieve our true potential.'

In public or in private, all of us are wrestling with life's complexity – from how to negotiate a relationship to how to pay the bills. Responding to others with kindness will never make things worse, and often make them better.

'The world,' runs a luminous phrase buried in the Book of Psalms, 'is built of kindness.' 'When you get dressed,' said the early Christian writer Paul, 'clothe yourselves with kindness.'

'Kindness,' said the Prophet Muhammad, 'is a mark of faith, and whoever is not kind has no faith.'

This is less about spontaneous acts ignited by compassion or indignation, and more a decision to follow a way of life signposted by mercy, generosity and justice. It's less about a breaking emotional wave and more about a steady, reliable tide of good action.

'Kindness is like water,' says the Dalai Lama, 'religion like tea.'

Come again?

In *An Appeal to the World: Ethics Are More Important than Religion* he describes how the tea we drink is made mostly of water, but it also contains other ingredients to make it taste good. But, however we make it, the main ingredient of tea is always water. And when push comes to shove, we can live without tea, but not without water. Likewise, he says, 'we are born without religion, but not without the basic need for compassion'.

In other words, while the human race could probably survive without religion, we don't stand a chance without kindness.

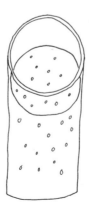

KNOW YOUR PLACE

Ever since humans exchanged a nomadic, hunter-gatherer existence for a settled agricultural one, location – place – has become more significant.

As hamlets have morphed into villages, towns, cities and nation states, place and identity have become more intertwined. Many people still see themselves bound to where they were born, or where they live. Even those of us whose education or career remove us from our foundations, often feel a sense of attachment to the place we came from.

But it's also possible to replant, to ground ourselves in a new location. The writer of the Hebrew Book of Proverbs said: 'By wisdom a house is built, and through understanding it is established; through knowledge its rooms are filled with rare and beautiful treasures.' We settle.

The shepherd Amanda Owen talks about how a group of hill sheep in the Yorkshire Dales will stick to their own patch of moorland – as their mothers did and their lambs will continue to – despite there being no boundaries to stop them from roaming. 'The word for this is "heafing". The sheep are "heafed" or "hefted" or "hoofed" on to their part of the moors.'

With her husband and nine children, she farmed Ravenseat, 2,000 acres with 1,000 sheep, alongside chickens, pigs, cows and horses. She talks of the almost spiritual rootedness she felt to the place: 'the sheep are heafed to Ravenseat, and so too I am attached to the place by an invisible bond'.

The Trappist monk Thomas Merton, who wrote about his intimacy with the woods that surrounded his hermitage in Kentucky, said: 'It is essential to experience all the times and moods of one good place.'

A deep satisfaction comes with finding a location with meaning. Even if it's your bedroom. At the turn of the seventeenth and eighteenth centuries, Xavier de Maistre wrote *A Journey Around My Room* in which, wearing pink and blue pyjamas, he would move from his bed to the sofa, and from his sofa to his desk as if he was embarking on a voyage of intrepid discovery.

It's good to feel earthed, a gift to have a place you can call home.

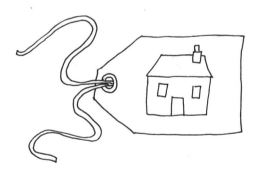

LIVE YOUR OWN LIFE

Dr Samuel Johnson once famously said, 'Depend upon it, sir, when a man knows he is to be hanged in a fortnight, it concentrates his mind wonderfully.' He was responding to the imminent execution of his friend William Dodd. The phrase has echoed across the generations.

There's nothing like impending death to clarify the thinking. Death does more than remind us to get our affairs in order: it invites us to ask what we really want from the time that we have left.

Sometimes that leads to regret about what we did with our time. We might even remember reaching a crossroads and wonder wistfully about the road we didn't follow.

Nowhere are those regrets more poignant than in the care home, where people live out their final days. In her conversations with patients in palliative care over a period of twelve years, Australian nurse Bronnie Ware noticed some common threads. People wished that they'd let themselves be happier in life. They regretted losing touch with friends. They felt sad for the times when they hadn't said what they'd been thinking – been unable to express their true feelings. Men, especially, said if they had their time again, they wouldn't spend so much of it at work.

All of these disappointments were summed up in the most common regret: 'I wish I'd had the courage to live a life true to myself, not the life others expected of me.'

It's no longer the gallows that will concentrate our minds about life, but it may well be a serious illness or a traumatic event that is the epiphany casting new light on our ordinary days. Towards the end of his life, Raymond Carver wrote a short biographical poem, 'Gravy', which is inscribed on his tombstone. It's the story of a man nearly dead from alcohol abuse at forty who 'changed his ways somehow'. The rest of his life, he wrote, was 'pure gravy'.

Although Carver died from lung cancer only ten years later, they were years of sobriety, love and happiness. At the junction he had taken a different road. He had no regrets.

We may recall our decisions at major crossroads but forget the minor ones, the myriad intersections of B-roads, cycle paths and holloways that sketch the ordnance survey map of any given day. The choices which shape who we become.

Speaking to graduates of Syracuse University, the novelist George Saunders reflected on how age invites us to wonder at the lives we didn't live. It wasn't strange jobs or disabling illness that he regretted, but how he'd responded to a small, shy stranger, briefly part of his class at school, routinely ignored and often teased. Forty years on, her hurt look still haunted his memory.

'What I regret most in my life are failures of kindness. Those moments when another human being was there, in front of me, suffering, and I responded … sensibly. Reservedly. Mildly.'

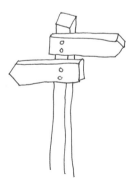

BREATHE IN

Air is our medium, like water is for fish. We can't live without it, but we take it for granted. Unless, for some reason, we can't breathe: submerged in water; choking; experiencing an asthma attack.

We notice air when it's moving, when we feel the breeze, or when a gust bowls a dustbin down the street. And air carries other things with it: the waft of perfume from someone's neck; the tang of brine from the ocean; the haze of woodsmoke from a cottage chimney.

But air is mostly about breath. It's what keeps us alive. When we breathe in, we exchange the oxygen for carbon dioxide and then breathe out. It's a life-giving rhythm. When we inhale, the air travels down our windpipe and into our lungs, it ends up in air sacs with thin walls called alveoli, from where the oxygen is absorbed into the bloodstream. Air becomes an indivisible part of us.

The early chapters of Genesis, the first book of the Bible, picture air in a more mystical way. At the dawn of creation, a divine wind sweeps over the face of the deep. The Hebrew word used for wind is also used for breath.

God *breathed* the world into being.

She *exhaled* it into existence.

God breathed life into the nostrils of humankind.

The first thing the first human did was to breathe in – and be inspired. It's pretty much the first thing any of us do when we're born.

We inhale through all our senses, taking in smells, sights, sounds, tastes, textures. We absorb what's in the air: ideas, stories, images, music, styles, attitudes, behaviour.

This *in*-spiration shapes who we are and what we do.

And who we are inspires others.

We breathe in and breathe out.

All of us, together.

In.

Out.

In.

Out.

Noticing our breathing, becoming mindful of it, helps us notice everything else. Thinking of nothing else is how we can think of everything.

Inspiration fills our lungs, but also our mind, our heart, our spirit.

What inspires us becomes who we are.

Breathing out, we become what we do.

UNPLUG YOURSELF

On the album *Kid A*, Radiohead recorded a song called 'How to Disappear Completely'. A few years later, they tried to do just that. Their website faded to blank and their social platforms were erased, except for a mysterious Instagram clip: a clay model of a chirping blackbird.

The blackbird featured in a video for a new song and Radiohead's absence was a marketing ruse designed to underline their presence. You can only reappear if you've disappeared.

Disappearing is more difficult than it used to be. It's harder to get away when we're all wired up to each other. Some days all our links feel like a chain.

When he was asked why he wasn't on email, the Irish writer John O'Donohue replied that he didn't want to return from a walk in the hills and find seventy people waiting for him in the kitchen. (Eventually, he gave in, his kitchen soon heaving like everyone else's.)

At one time we could disappear into a good book, but now, a smartphone looks longingly at us, begging to break the spell of the story we're in. When a teenager fails to return a text her parents fear the worst, forgetting that such instant connection didn't exist when they were kids themselves. A time when they might have disappeared for hours before anyone became concerned.

But an intentional disappearance can be transformative. Just as a good sleep can help the mind untangle a knot of thoughts, so the act of disconnection can spark better connections.

'Almost everything will work again if you unplug it for a few minutes,' says Anne Lamott. 'Including you.'

As Jesus of Nazareth said on one of his own periodic disappearing days, 'Come apart to a deserted place by yourself and rest.'

Which, being translated, means: 'Log off.'

Tell your phone it's nothing personal as you pop it in a drawer.

Go for a wander with no destination in mind.

Vanish into the diary you wanted to write.

Push open the door of an empty, silent church.

Disconnect, and disappear.

Unplug yourself.

Just for an hour or two.

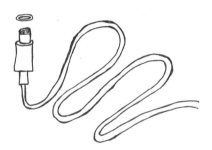

I AM BECAUSE YOU ARE

'To be is to do' (Socrates)
'To do is to be' (Sartre)
'Do be do be do' (Sinatra)

This was how novelist Kurt Vonnegut summed up our existential quest to answer the biggest questions. The seventeenth-century French philosopher René Descartes came up with his own pithy aphorism to explain who and why we are: 'I think, therefore I am.'

He didn't make the cut in the Vonnegut joke, but René found himself in another one, in which he walks into a bar and is asked if he'd like a beer. 'I think not,' he replies ... and promptly disappears.

Do we live in our heads? Or in our daily actions? How do we even know we're here? Enlightenment thinkers like Descartes were not just big on reason but also on individualism, an influence that shapes our twenty-first- century world of capitalism, commerce and consumption. A world captured in another sound bite: 'I shop, therefore I am.'

Individualism also informs what we talk about when we talk about the divine. How do I get to heaven? Why do I feel bad about myself? How do I become a better person? But in southern Africa a Bantu word – *ubuntu* – suggests an alternative way of answering the big questions.

Ubuntu can best be translated as 'I am because you are'. It's a word that signals how each of us finds our best self only in relationship to others. How life is not to be understood as a solitary, individual pursuit but as something we share. That we understand ourselves better when we live in company not alone. That we can't be human on our own.

'*Ubuntu* speaks about the fact that you can't exist as a human being in isolation,' said Archbishop Desmond Tutu. We're interconnected not simply individuals. Whatever we do affects someone else.

This is counter-intuitive in a culture where our goals often centre on personal fulfilment, in family or career. In spirituality and religion. But many of our deepest questions can't be answered in isolation, only in friendship. Many of them ('why is there so much suffering?') can barely be answered at all. We have to live with these questions. But living with them with others sometimes means we become the answers ourselves.

Those others might be a lonely neighbour, an annoying relative, a sick child, an estranged partner. Or they might be losing hope in Syria, locked up in Guantánamo, forgotten in Gaza. They might be the people we meet when we hesitatingly volunteer at that rough sleepers' hostel – or step over the threshold of a local synagogue, mosque, or church.

Religion is not solitary but communal. Do it on your own and chances are you'll give up, but a virtue in being part of a faith community is that on the days when you're mainly full of doubt, someone else can believe on your behalf.

And there might even be the odd day when you're the one with enough faith when someone else has none.

It's not about you.

It's about us.

To be is to be together.

'I am because you are.'

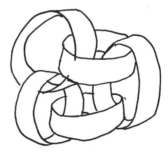

FAIL AGAIN

In 1993, when the Dual Cyclone vacuum cleaner arrived, people praised the genius of inventor James Dyson. Dyson had been less celebrated in the previous fifteen years when he had come up with 5,126 machines, before the one that worked. 'But I learned from each one,' he said. 'That's how I came up with a solution. So I don't mind failure.'

Dyson's failures made him.

Considering that it's endured by anyone who is successful, failure gets a bad press. The business ideas that didn't take off … before the one that did. The rejection letters to (later) famous authors. The fabled gigs with seven in the audience of (later) bestselling bands.

The path of failure can also lead to a success we weren't seeking. When you're next spraying lubricant on a creaking door hinge, take a moment to give thanks to Dr Norm Larsen of the Rocket Chemical Company. Norm was not thinking door hinges. He was thinking of creating a formula to stop corrosion in nuclear missiles. But Norm failed. Then Norm failed again. Norm failed thirty-nine times until finally his snappily titled 'Water Displacement' product came good at the fortieth attempt. But no one thinks less of Norm's WD-40 because WD-1 to WD-39 were failures.

Dashed hopes, thwarted plans or mistaken calculations can be paradoxically illuminating. A counter-intuitive thought in a note from the biblical letter-writer Paul puts it like this: 'Power is made perfect in weakness.'

The story of scientific understanding is one of blind alleys and failed experiments, of reversing up dead-end streets to think again. The entire scientific method is based on the notion of discovering what does not work as much as finding what does.

Every day is trial and error, which is how, when we reflect, we come to understand ourselves and learn to relate to each other.

Maybe schoolchildren, says James Dyson, should be marked by the number of failures they've had. Maybe those who try strange things and experience lots of failures to get there are more creative.

'Make glorious and fantastic mistakes,' said the writer Neil Gaiman to a class of graduating students. 'Leave the world more interesting for your being here.'

Every hesitant folly or bold failure helps us refine the experiment we call our life. 'Ever tried. Ever failed,' said playwright Samuel Beckett. 'No matter. Try Again. Fail again. Fail better.'

SAY A LITTLE PRAYER

The impulse to pray goes back further than organised religion.

It's a human instinct – the desire to seek help in a time of trouble or give thanks when life is good.

And while certain kinds of prayer look for a direct divine connection, not all prayer does.

Uttering a prayer can also act as a note to self. Just as writers often say that writing something down helps them understand what they think, so people in therapy will say that expressing their feelings in a safe environment gives them a new way of understanding themselves.

Saying a prayer – writing it down, speaking it out – can do something similar. It can bring us clarity. Or help us reconsider. Or offer resolution.

The Old English word 'Amen' – the full stop at the end of many prayers – is the act of affirmation that says: 'make it so'.

Write your own prayers.

Speak them out.

Make it so.

This one's for you, sitting opposite me. Whatever it is you need, I hope you get it. (And let's hope that someone, today, will send one out for me.) **Amen.**

For that last breath. And this next one. For this heart, which keeps on beating even though I never notice. For being here. For being alive. Thanks. **Amen.**

I wonder where she's from. Originally. The life she left behind. I couldn't be doing what she's doing, unless I was desperate. God help her. **Amen.**

I can't stand this job. There, I've said it. I need to change something. I need to make a new start. Maybe today. So. Help. Me. **Amen.**

I shouldn't have said that. Something snapped. I lost it. I sometimes do. He was wrong. But all the same, so was I. Sorry about that. I mean it. **Amen.**

This is me wishing things were different. Wishing the world well. Wishing you well. Today. Saying a prayer. **Amen.**

I'm not going to let this wind me up. Someone, somewhere is facing something far more serious. God help them. (And me too while you're at it.) **Amen.**

Thanks for her. And for them. For her wise words and their kind smile. Thank you, people. You know who you are. **Amen.**

LET'S TAKE A WALK

Life is sometimes compared to a journey. (Quite often actually.) At decisive moments we see ourselves at a 'crossroads'. We talk of 'the onward march of history' as if there is some greater superhighway taken by the whole human race, a voyage underway long before we showed up which will continue long after we've left.

Make this journey as part of a faith community, and sometimes we recall being given a map. Sitting down at our metaphorical roadside, we unpack our sandwiches and flask of tea and spread out this map. Unfortunately, as the poet Stephen Levine put it, while Buddha, Jesus and Krishna each left maps of a kind, 'you still have to travel the road yourself'.

Some people have a clear destination in mind, and a short-cut to get there. The answer to 'the ultimate question of life, the universe and everything is 42' wrote Douglas Adams in *The Hitchhiker's Guide to the Galaxy*. Some people don't get the joke, that there isn't anything as tawdry as an 'answer'. That there is no accurate map and, anyway, the place we're looking for can never be pinpointed. 'It is not down on any map,' wrote Herman Melville in *Moby Dick*. 'True places never are.'

But still, the journey.

In London since 1865, Hackney carriage – and then black cab – drivers have been obliged to complete 'the Knowledge', which involves several years' training in the city's eccentric jigsaw of highways and byways.

The arrival of the satnav put the cabbie on the endangered species list.

But if information may displace knowledge on our roads, on our metaphorical journey speed is not of the essence; the wisdom of tried-and-trusted experience will not be overtaken. Sometimes we need to take the scenic route, even if it makes us late.

For this we need wise travelling companions, people who've been this way before. If we can see past their frailty or failing memory, we will notice such guides all around. They made their mistakes, but also, sometimes learnt from them.

They are often referred to as 'old people'.

To our information society they bring wisdom, which is why, in many cultures, they are not dismissed as 'past their sell by' but revered as elders. 'Grey hair,' reads the Bible, 'is a crown of glory. Wisdom is with the aged.' Do not forsake wisdom, it adds, 'she will protect you; love her, and she will watch over you'.

If experience suggests that there is no 'answer' to life, no direct route to our destination, we may also recognise that the concept of truth will not be reduced to information or mathematical formula. That a film or a poem can also be true, a friend can be true, even a way of life. 'To believe in God,' said Ludwig Wittgenstein, 'is to know that the facts of the world are not the end of the matter.'

We take most of our questions along with us on the way and we make the way by walking. A Latin phrase is as good a motto for the journey as any: *solvitur ambulando* – it is solved by walking.

From the meaning of life to the problem of pain, from our broken relationships to our longing for love, answers are few and far between. Some days we just keep on keeping on.

Some days it is solved by walking.

TAKE A DAY OFF

Vesak
Diwali
Eid al-Fitr
Pesach
Christmas
Parinirvana Day
Holi
Hanukkah
Easter
Eid al-Adha

There are more. Hinduism alone has a thousand plus.

Holy days.

From which we get our more common 'holiday'.

And to which we might add less sacred versions like Duvet Day and Throwing of a Sickie Day.

Everyone needs a day off.

According to the creation story recorded in the Bible, even God needed a lie-down after slogging away all week in creating the cosmos. 'And he rested on the seventh day from all his work which he had made.'

Out of this grew traditions in Judaism, Islam and Christianity about setting aside a weekly 'sabbath'.

A day of rest.

Religious holy days may be rooted in founders' birthdays and lunar and seasonal cycles; at grassroots level they're often an excuse for some well-earned R & R. The busier our days, the more essential our rest days.

'We humans have lost the wisdom of genuinely resting and relaxing,' said Buddhist monk Thich Nhat Hanh. We worry too much, he adds, which means we don't allow our bodies, our minds and our hearts to heal.

The ancient practices of good religion can be reminders of how to live a good life. As nature teaches us, rest is vital for regeneration. The poet Ovid landed it: 'A field that has rested gives a more beautiful crop.'

It's about looking after ourselves, said Maya Angelou. 'We all need to withdraw from the cares that will not withdraw from us.'

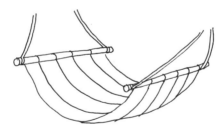

MAKE BIG DECISIONS SLOWLY

Is he the one? Can I commit?
If they offer it, should I take it?
I've got to say something, but how shall I put it?
It's a lot of money ... is it worth it?
Is that really what I want to do with my life?

Decisions punctuate our waking hours. Most are so routine we barely notice we're making them. Some are so significant they may shape the career we pursue, or the person we spend our days with.

It's said we make 35,000 decisions every day – over 200 just on food. Most are snap judgements drawing on intuition, experience and simple reasoning: 'No sugar, thanks.' But sometimes, reaching a resolution requires time because the consequences may be life-changing: 'I do.'

The Jesuit priest James Martin suggests that before starting to think through a decision we should try to be 'indifferent'. He doesn't mean not giving a damn, but finding a sense of detachment and freedom. Step back from the emotions stirred up by a particular quandary and choose to be impartial.

If we can gain some kind of detachment, then we can imaginatively follow the route of a decision in a certain direction. Or the other.

Living with that person, how does that feel? Or deciding to live with them ... no longer.

The Jesuits draw on the teachings of the fifteenth-century Christian mystic Ignatius of Loyola, who said that in making decisions we should look for signs in our feelings of 'consolation', or 'desolation'.

A job opportunity, for example, may mean more money and leaping several rungs up a career ladder. It may be a great choice. But if the thought of it leaves you feeling empty, disappointed with yourself – *desolate* – then maybe this job is not quite who you are. Alternatively, if the prospect leaves you with 'a sense of rightness, of peace' – if it leaves you feeling *consoled* – perhaps it would be a move in the right direction.

In big decisions, Ignatius suggested it helps if you remind yourself of your ultimate objectives in life – the kind of person you want to become. Or to imagine yourself at the end of your life: what would the late and wise version of yourself think about this decision? Would they intervene on behalf of this person being unfairly bad-mouthed? Would they make this investment of time or money? Would they put up with this troubling situation?

What would your 'best self' do?

How would the person that you long to be make this choice?

However reliable our instincts, it's wise not to rush into making big decisions. It's wise to imaginatively practise alternative futures, to try them on for size. It's wise to line up the pros and cons … and then to sleep on them.

'Make big decisions slowly, and small decisions fast,' says God, when he turns up for a chat in the kitchen, in a poem by Anthony Wilson.

It's wise to sit quietly, and listen to your deepest self.

Now and again, the decision will be made for you.

PAUSE. REMEMBER. GIVE THANKS. EAT.

At one time, when people stopped their daily routine for a meal, they would give thanks. In cultures steeped in Christian history, this was called saying grace.

Asking a blessing on the food.

But mealtimes metamorphosed as working patterns changed. Now, we eat on the run, or in front of a screen. Alone, rather than in families. New rituals displace old ones. People may still pause religiously before a meal … to snap a photo of the food and Instagram it.

If the earlier ritual was about connecting with the divine, the new one is about connecting with each other. Perhaps it's because our relationship with food has changed.

At one time we produced our own food, or traded it with a neighbour. As in many developing countries today, most people were smallholders – everyday life rooted in the earth, the soil producing the food which kept everyone alive. Or didn't. Harvest time was precarious, which explains that famous line in that famous prayer: 'Give us this day our daily bread.'

But we have become separated from the ground beneath our feet, from the earth that delivers our food and the people who produce it. By the time we eat our breakfast, said Martin Luther King Jr in the 1960s, we've depended 'on half the world'. The world has been shrinking every day since, and now a local shop may have every country on its shelves.

Our fruit and veg comes shrink-wrapped and protected for travel. We don't see the journey it made to reach us. We don't see Agnes plucking these pears for us in South Africa, or Mary in St Lucia cropping those bananas, or Blaise in Ghana sorting these tomatoes.

We don't notice and so we forget to be grateful.

'Dear God,' as Bart Simpson once put it before a meal, 'we paid for all this stuff ourselves, so thanks for nothing!'

We take for granted those who produce our food and we can be complacent about the variety and reliability of our food supply. But giving thanks is good:

To God if you believe in her.

Or to those invisible people in the supply chain who harvested our food.

Or to those visible people who produced it, in our kitchen.

Or served us, in the restaurant.

Mealtimes are the perfect lay-by in the daily race, allowing us to pause, reflect and give thanks.

To say grace, as they used to say.

Or simply to hold a moment of silent gratitude.

BREAK BREAD

Think of the extraordinary number of different shapes and forms it comes in. Crusty French sticks, all airy in the middle; warm doughy naan; Arabic flatbread; pizza; damp white slices built for a bacon sarnie. Challah, anyone?

Bread is wonderful.

Bread is a staple for many people across the globe. No wonder that it's become a powerful metaphor. It stands for something elemental. Bread comes out of an organic process of life and death: the seed goes into the ground and dies. It is reborn as wheat, then cut down, and the grain ground into flour. Then yeast brings it alive once more, as the goodness of the grain is released in the making and baking.

We eat, and excrete and it returns to the earth. It's a life cycle.

'All bread,' writes Margaret Atwood: '… is made of wood, cow dung, packed brown moss, the bodies of dead animals …'

'Bread is the staff of life', as the saying goes.

Jesus of Nazareth called himself 'the bread of life' and in the Christian rite of Eucharist people share bread and say: 'Though we are many, we are one body, because we all share in one bread.'

Whatever we believe, food brings us together.

The word 'company' – from the Latin *cum* ('with') and *panis* ('bread') – means sharing bread.

A companion is someone you share bread with.

A company is a group that eats together. We all share in one bread. The bread has to be broken to share it. Together, says Atwood, we eat this earth.

Food is a binding agent, a social glue. Sharing food is the heart of hospitality. The welcoming of the stranger is common to cultures and religions the world over. Breaking bread, and the conversation that comes with it, breaks down barriers.

Turns strangers into friends.

Bread is wonderful.

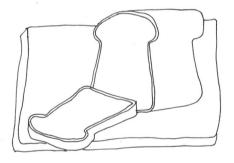

WHAT DO YOU PLAN TO DO?

A woman lies under the summer sun, soaking up the rays.

Slowly, she becomes aware that she is not alone, the faintest of movement on her hand.

A tiny grasshopper has landed. The precision of its movement and fragile beauty gives her a sense of the wonder of every day, the passing of time itself.

Such an ordinary moment proved an unlikely epiphany for the Pulitzer-winning poet Mary Oliver, sparking the deepest of questions in her poem 'The Summer Day'.

'Tell me, what is it you plan to do/with your one wild and precious life?'

It's a fine thing to lie under the sun and watch the world go by but the sun goes down, and when it rises we have to get back to work and pay for the roof over our heads.

But work is more than paying the bills. It's how we make our mark in life. How we were here, and how we made the most of it. The evidence on our CV is what columnist David Brooks, in *The Road to Character*, calls our 'résumé virtues' – accomplishments in education and career that witness our external achievements in this life; that signal our status. From exam results to progress at the company, the skills we develop and our take-home salary.

But, as the saying goes, nobody will say on their deathbed, 'I wish I'd spent more time at the office.'

And Brooks noticed another set of virtues, the values he found in people who radiated an inner light. This parallel set of qualifications he called 'eulogy virtues' – what people might say about you when you die.

At your funeral, no one will mention the hours you put in at work, your title or salary. They will remember another edition of your life.

He was a father who loved playing with his kids.

She was a neighbour who'd always ask after your health.

She was generous and patient.

They were loyal and brave.

You could trust her.

Eulogy virtues are hard to measure, but easier to witness. They're not about your qualifications in life but the quality of your life. They are a glue that holds families and friendships together, that help us negotiate life's toughest tests.

The best eulogy recalls someone who recognised their human flaws, and tried to face them down.

Are we mean or consumed with envy?

Do we hold grudges?

Can we compromise?

Can we forgive?

Do we ever shut up and let others speak?

Building a career 'out there' is no substitute for building character 'in here'.

The danger of the passing years is that we may fail to find a 'moral vocabulary', fail to dive deep into our souls and so conclude that as long as we're relatively decent we've done OK.

That our life will be measured by what we did, rather than who we became.

But we're not here for long.

Witness the grasshopper.

Next time one lands on your hand.

TAKE THE OVERVIEW

There are 7.5 billion of us sharing this planet. We live on seven continents, connected by five oceans. We speak 6,000 languages, with Mandarin Chinese the most popular (1.2 billion speakers) or English, if you include those who speak a second language.

We disagree over everything: from how to organise society to which football team to support; from our religious traditions to the food we eat. We can be suspicious and fearful – of people of another colour, or sexual orientation, or culture.

Ever since Cain and Abel (sons of the mythical first family of Adam and Eve) had a domestic dispute, and Cain murdered Abel, we've turned to violence to win our arguments. We're not good at peaceful resolution of disputes. According to *The New York Times*, humans have been entirely at peace for only 268 years in the past 3,400 – that's 8 per cent of recorded history: 'Estimates for the total number killed in wars throughout all of human history range from 150 million to 1 billion.'

Perhaps we need to take a breath.

Get some perspective.

Take a different view of this planet we share.

For the first time in history, we can get one.

In 1987 the writer Frank White, after speaking with twenty-nine astronauts, came up with the 'overview effect' theory.

Seeing Earth from space, he argued, transforms both how we understand ourselves and how we see our world. The astronaut begins to think of Earth as a 'shared home' and develops a sense of awe.

Edgar Mitchell, an astronaut on Apollo 14, described his emotions as 'interconnected euphoria'. Something happens to you out there, he said, you develop an almost instant global, people-oriented view of the planet which gives rise to an intense dissatisfaction with the state of the world, and a compulsion to do something about it.

'From out there on the moon, international politics look so petty. You want to grab a politician by the scruff of the neck and drag him a quarter of a million miles out and say, "Look at that, you son of a bitch."'

William Anders, one of the first three people to have left Earth's orbit and travel to the moon, got just such an overview.

'We came all this way to explore the moon, and the most important thing is that we discovered the Earth.'

LIVE YOUR WAY INTO A NEW KIND OF THINKING

In the twenty-first century, the great faith traditions are caught up in a long-running argument over what their adherents believe. People of faith are notable not because of what they do, but because of what they believe. Or don't.

Are they comfortable with gay, lesbian and trans people? Do women have the same rights as men? Is there a dress code? Do miracles happen? Do the findings of science contradict religion? Or complement it? Is a holy book prescriptive? Or for general guidance?

Take Christianity. The Church has taught that if we can get our beliefs right then we'll be able to get our actions right. Orthodoxy leads to orthopraxis. Otherwise there will be weeping and gnashing of teeth, which will require orthodontistry.

The Church is big on crossing the Ts and dotting the Is. While religion often oversells doctrine it often undersells community and friendship.

Community activist Ann Morisy noticed that Jesus didn't say that he spoke, or believed, the way, he said 'I am the way.' He didn't say that he'd speak true words or tell us about the truth, but, 'I am the truth'.

He saw truth in relationships and friendship, not in facts and dogma. If you wanted to know truth you needed to become friends, and the community of those friends eventually got called 'Church'.

Tempting though it is for educated people to argue about religion, the benefits of faith are found not in the speculating but in the participating.

Not in the theory but in the practical.

It's better to *do* religion than to *think* religion.

And practising is the only way to believe it.

If you can't believe your way into faith, you can practise your way.

This was captured by the Dutch writer Henri Nouwen who said: 'You don't think your way into a new kind of living. You live your way into a new kind of thinking.'

LIGHT IS STRONGER THAN DARKNESS

'It's better to light a candle than to curse the darkness.'

Well, up to a point.

Cursing the darkness can be quite therapeutic. Unleashing a primal scream. Letting it all out. Howling at the moon.

But the benefits may be short term. Ultimately, the darkness is pretty resistant to insults and cursing. The darkness is often faceless, nameless, random and not open to negotiation.

But still, darkness falls.

Our lives can put us in the way of devastating sadness. From the sudden death of a friend to an inexplicable act of violence on our streets. From a downswing in our mental wellbeing to the traumatic end of a cherished relationship.

Days, weeks and months can become too difficult to process. If we ever did have words to express the deep ache of sadness we feel – for ourselves or for someone else – they long ago started sounding empty and we're tired of speaking them.

Yet even when life is pitch dark, we want to believe that it is not the end of the story.

If we don't have the words to describe how we feel, or to chart a way out, we have metaphors and none more elemental than that of light and dark.

This is why, after the shocking terror attack, people gather together in town squares after dark and light candles.

And why solidarity for a group of people under threat or facing disaster is signalled by a candlelight vigil.

Why people queue solemnly at places of worship to add one more flickering flame to a shimmering field of illuminated candles.

And why it's not a futile gesture to light a candle in our own homes, when friends gather – to declare companionship with each other, and to help find a way through the darkness.

A small, frail, wordless act of resistance in favour of life.

As Archbishop Desmond Tutu, whose life was spent campaigning against the darkness of apartheid, put it: 'Goodness is stronger than evil. Love is stronger than hate. Light is stronger than darkness. Life is stronger than death.'

WE ARE NOT ALONE

'The Lord is my shepherd; I shall not want.

He maketh me to lie down in green pastures: he leadeth me beside the still waters.

He restoreth my soul: he leadeth me in the paths of righteousness for his name's sake.

Yea, though I walk through the valley of the shadow of death, I will fear no evil: for thou art with me; thy rod and thy staff they comfort me.

Thou preparest a table before me in the presence of mine enemies: thou anointest my head with oil; my cup runneth over.

Surely goodness and mercy shall follow me all the days of my life: and I will dwell in the house of the Lord for ever.'

It's the go-to poem for people feeling fragile or raw, broken or lost.

Psalm 23 is the Bible offering us a consoling arm over the shoulder. And it works. That's why it's read so often at funerals.

It's honest.

While life has green pastures and still waters, beyond them lurks the presence of enemies and the valley of the shadow of death.

We get that.

But the ancient poet offers reassurance that whatever life throws at us – good or bad – we're never left entirely alone. The psalmist found her comfort in the watchful presence of a divine companion.

Companionship is solace.

When the birds sing and the river chuckles, we turn to our soul mates to share our pleasure. When night falls and wolves howl, we draw close to each other for comfort.

In company, we can still raise a glass, even if hostile faces press themselves against the window. Goodness and mercy are still around the table.

'Even when the way goes through Death Valley,' as the poet Eugene Peterson translates these verses in *The Message*, 'I'm not afraid when you walk at my side.'

'Your beauty and love chase after me every day of my life.'

Amen, as the psalmist would say.

PLAY IT BACK

The philosopher Plato, living around 400 years before Jesus of Nazareth, recorded the words of another philosopher, Socrates, who had said: 'The unexamined life is not worth living.'

Maybe Socrates was exaggerating to make a point, but a lot of people seem perfectly happy not putting their passing days under a microscope.

Perhaps we fear what we might find. Maybe, at one time, we did stop to look.

Or we believe we're too busy for self-reflection. It's on the list – for later.

Perhaps we see ourselves as more about action than reflection, more *doing* than *being*.

But others find that an examined life can be surprisingly rewarding: taking a moment to stop and notice what we're doing with our time.

A day contains 1,440 minutes.

Putting aside five for a moment of review may transform the other 1,435.

A practice like this might be called meditation, or mindfulness.

It might be called prayer.

The Jesuits, a religious order founded by Ignatius of Loyola in the sixteenth century, picked up early on the idea of a daily playback. Ignatius created a series of spiritual exercises designed to help people deepen their experience. One of these – conducting a slo-mo replay of the day's action – can enrich anyone's life. It's often called 'the Examen', or a 'consciousness examination'. A simple, daily life check.

The kind of exercise we can do each night before bed; reminding ourselves that this day, like all the rest, is a bit of a jigsaw. Considering the shape of some of the pieces might help us put it all together. Examining our life might help shape it.

'How we spend our days is how we spend our lives,' as Annie Dillard writes.

The Examen has five steps:

Give thanks. Replay the day you've had, freeze-frame the people or moments you're grateful for.

Capture some sign of hope or joy. Was there a moment of forgiveness or compassion? A sign of courage or unexpected love? We often notice these moments only in retrospect.

Notice any sadness or regret. Some news you heard about or event you were part of? Some word you regret or action you neglected?

Recognise the down as well as the up. Acknowledge the bad as well as the good.

Consider tomorrow. In light of all this, how might it be different?

Rewind.

Hit play.

Watch the day again.

What was good, what was not?

Examine your life.

There is no test. Life is all coursework.

TRAVEL LIGHT

Who can predict the course of a life?

Is it written in the stars?

A hidden hand in history or blind fate?

From where most of us are standing, it looks like we have to make it up as we go along.

To play the hand we're dealt.

If life is a journey, none of us carry the same things in our rucksack. Each of us is a product of so many factors: location, timing, culture, genes, upbringing, education, peers, personality, chance, choice and faith … or the lack of it.

We set off, not quite knowing where we're going to until we get there.

'Life can only be understood backwards,' as philosopher Søren Kierkegaard put it, 'but it must be lived forwards.'

Our ambitions change as we discover our strengths and weaknesses. So do our beliefs and codes of practice – those absorbed from our family and background – as experience helps us understand ourselves and our life.

In late adolescence we can pass through what another philosopher, Paul Ricoeur, calls a 'desert of criticism', when we re-examine our ideas, even our identity. But on the other side of that desert, having reshaped some of our ideas, our conclusions may remain provisional.

We may lose our purpose in life … or finally find it.

Lose our faith … or find it.

We course-correct as we live, our travelling plans subverted by unpredicted events or unexpected opportunities. The person we fancy doesn't fancy us back. Someone offers us a job. We have a baby. 'We make plans and God laughs,' as the Yiddish proverb runs.

We input new coordinates and reset the satnav. We travel on.

We look for meaning and completeness. The journey takes on a religious quality, even if we don't use that language.

A quest. A kind of pilgrimage.

We make the journey up as we go along, taking sustenance from what we pick up on the way. We can't see the whole picture and never land on some unified theory of everything. We probably couldn't deal with it, even if we did.

We take directions from fellow travellers, from signposts, from our own internal compass.

We learn to adapt.

We learn to travel light.

Novelist Ursula K. Le Guin, summed it up: 'It is good to have an end to journey toward; but it is the journey that matters, in the end.'

STAND STILL

Saint Kevin was a hermit who lived in Glendalough, County Wicklow in the sixth century.

His cell was so small that when he prayed, with arms outstretched, he had to stick one of them out of the window.

One day, while Kevin was absorbed in prayerful contemplation, a blackbird landed on his hand. It was a long prayer and Kevin was standing so still that the bird started to build a nest in Kevin's palm.

Which was a problem when he'd finished his prayers.

Should he drop the nest or just keep standing there? With his arm sticking out? Being a saint, he decided to keep standing there.

For weeks.

The blackbird laid her eggs and hatched them and fed her chicks.

And eventually the young fledged and flew the nest and Kevin … relaxed.

The story echoes the poetry of William Blake who wrote about holding 'infinity in the palm of your hand and eternity in an hour'.

Rooted to the spot, Kevin became a kind of tree, the circle of life, death and rebirth held in his branches.

Kevin grew into a prayer.

Wildlife photographers and other nature-watchers talk about a quality of stillness which enables them to disappear so that the life around becomes more fully itself.

The standing still is emptying.

And it's also receiving.

The Hebrew prophet Elijah, standing outside his cave, was listening for the voice of God in a thunderstorm or an earthquake or a fire. To his surprise, he found it in 'a sound of sheer silence'.

Maybe, suggested the poet Pablo Neruda, if we stopped for a second and didn't move our arms so much, 'a huge silence' would interrupt us.

IMAGINE IT

Human beings are makers. We invent stuff: tools, machines, meals, stories, art, religions, cultures, mischief. At some indeterminate and debated-over point in ancient prehistory our creative capacity took off in what historian Yuval Noah Harari calls a 'cognitive revolution'. And creation is one of the things that marks us out.

The engine of making is the imagination. And the fuel of that engine is a question:

What if?

A question that sends us way beyond straightforward invention:

What if I were you?

In order for us to understand one another, we need to imagine what it's like to be the other. Otherwise we do one another harm, trample over each others' feelings.

To deliberately hurt someone is a failure of the imagination. When we cry at weddings, view movies, watch our children play, we are imagining life through someone else's eyes.

Wouldn't it work better if?

It takes imagination to plan anything: to develop a road system; to make a garden; to choose a school for our kids; to decide how much garlic to add to the casserole. To think ahead.

Could we possibly?

Our ability to hope is embedded in the imagination. Anne Frank, Nelson Mandela, Rachel Carson, Harvey Milk and Malala Yousafzai envisioned another, better world. Unless we can imagine that there is more than this, we're stuck in despair.

Is there more to life?

Faith and belief are not built on certainties but they're fired by imagination. For instance, thinking that there might be a God (or not), and trying to work out what that God might be like. That's why we use metaphors for the divine: a parent, a despot, a shepherd, a friend.

By definition God defies definition.

So even in our understanding of the sacred, there's an element of invention.

What would happen if?

Imagination opens us up to infinite possibilities.

What would happen if you asked?

What would happen if you kissed him?

What would happen if you stopped it?

What would happen if you set off?

What would happen if you … added some anchovy?

SHARE YOUR WINNINGS

You've got to be in it to win it.

It *could* be you.

The chances are you'll play it this week. Or someone in your family will. 70 per cent of people in the UK play the National Lottery regularly. They're betting that their number will come up. That luck will be on their side.

It's not logical. It's faith. Or maybe just fun.

The odds of winning the jackpot are 1 in 45 million. You are more likely to be hit by part of a plane falling from the sky (1 in 10 million), be crushed by a vending machine (1 in 112 million) or to die from flesh-eating bacteria (1 in 1 million).

We can't prove luck exists but we often behave as if it does. 'Good luck,' we say, as if it will make some kind of difference. 'Bad luck!' we commiserate – as if some unseen force explains why your horse fell at the last, or you unexpectedly lost your job.

Why do we think it could be us? Perhaps it's evolutionary. Perhaps it's because the odds of just being alive on this good earth, in this strange universe, are so much longer.

Someone with a lot of time on their hands calculated the odds of any of us being born at one in ten … followed by two and three-quarter million zeroes. In other words, the odds of being alive are so improbable that winning the lottery looks quite plausible. Just by being here all our numbers came up.

And we're luckier still.

We can send our children to school, call on a doctor when we're sick, vote out politicians we don't like.

Most of this good fortune was made by people who came before us, people who got lucky with their own health or education and decided to share their winnings by working for the rights we take for granted.

Religions find luck hard to explain. Faith and fate, divinity and destiny are not always good company. But whether we believe in God or don't, we lucked out just by being alive. Right here, right now.

FEAR NOT

Fear comes in all shapes and sizes.

It's at the heart of what it means to be human:

The fear of the unknown or of the known.
The fear of not being in control.
The fear of missing out, the fear of taking part.
The fear of loving, the fear of not loving.
The fear of losing love.
The fear of not being good enough.
The fear of someone else – at work or on the street.
The fear of illness, the fear of death.
The fear of never having lived.

We all carry fears, however secretly. However much we deny them.
Maybe it's some primal survival instinct but the suspicion is that we're
never quite safe and secure.

If we cannot banish our fears, we can make sure they don't banish us.
We don't have to be managed by fear and insecurity. There is no more
common phrase in the Bible than 'Have no fear'.

Or this: 'Do not be afraid.'

Fear not.

But how?

'The only way to ease our fear and be truly happy,' said the Buddhist monk Thich Nhat Hanh, 'is to acknowledge our fear and look deeply' at its source. Instead of trying to escape from our fear, we can turn to it, we can look at it clearly and deeply.

Fear makes us defensive, turns us in on ourselves. Its opposite is not courage, but love. Love accepts, includes, is symbolised by open arms.

'There is no fear in love,' said the early Christian writer John, 'but perfect love casts out fear.'

THE LAW OF ONE

It's usually called the golden rule, and it turns up in many of the great religious traditions.

In Islam it appears like this: 'No one of you is a believer until he desires for his brother that which he desires for himself.'

In Buddhism: 'Hurt not others in ways that you yourself would find hurtful.'

In Confucianism: 'Do not do to others what you do not want them to do to you.'

In Judaism: 'What is hateful to you, do not do to your fellow man. This is the law: all the rest is commentary.'

In Hinduism: 'This is the sum of duty: do not do to others what would cause pain if done to you.'

Someone summed it up as 'the Law of One':

'We are all one. When one is harmed, all are harmed. When one is helped, all are helped.'

It's known as the ethic of reciprocity or, as Jesus of Nazareth put it: 'Do unto others as you'd have them do to you.'

While the idea is sanctified by religions, it's not owned by them. It's also cherished by people who don't buy religion at all. Putting yourself in someone else's shoes probably goes back before religion itself. And before shoes.

Empathy promotes kindness, compassion, understanding and respect. My decisions affect my neighbour – not just over the road but over the sea. On a neighbouring continent. Not just later today, but later in this century.

Everyone's connected when we all share one planet.

There's so many of us. And also ... just the one of us.

TRUST YOUR GUT

On the first day in a new job our antennae go into overload. Particularly with the people who share our new habitat. Every receptor is on alert for signals. Is she stuck-up or shy? Is he being friendly ... or over-compensating? Why does she do that thing with her hair? Is he being sarcastic? Do I like her? Can I trust him?

No one single sense is involved in these perceptions: it's all of them, at the same time. We get a reading off someone in an instant.

Call it gut instinct, intuition, a hunch.

Sometimes we just have a feeling.

These readings from people, places or situations aren't logical constructions. They don't come from slow reasoning; they arrive as a hit. But that doesn't mean we can't trust them. Our instinctive decryptions are a mash-up of our lived experience. Life speaking to us without words.

Sometimes our bad experiences can make us fearful, or defensive, and give us a false reading of someone. And other people's own insecurities can mean they jam their own signals. It's wise not to rush to judgement. But still, our instincts are pretty reliable and in the normal round of life, work and relationships, there's no time for the kind of vetting necessary to join the security services.

The singer Bono puts it like this: 'I've always believed in instinct over intellect. The instinct is what you always knew; intellect is what you figure out.' We take a leap of faith and, as essayist Malcolm Gladwell writes in *Blink*, 'There can be as much value in the blink of an eye as in months of rational analysis.'

We need to be able to put our trust in our instincts and in each other, even if it's provisional. Faith and instinct, says broadcaster Melvyn Bragg, are kissing cousins: 'I think faith is … like instinct, which I've always thought is compressed intelligence, at such a high speed you can't see it, as fast as a blink.'

And like instinct, he says, 'faith is very often a whole perception which has to be (as it were) deconstructed into what is plausible and what is not'.

We can lean on our instinct, this faith, we can lay bets on it. We have to, otherwise we can't make relationships. But we also need to interrogate it. Left unquestioned, instinct can become bigotry and phobia. But when our instincts warm us to people, to ideas, and ways of living, life unfurls like a bud under the sun.

TUNE IN

Four hundred years ago George Herbert wrote a poem about prayer, without explaining what prayer was. But in two words he hinted at what can happen when we pray.

'Something understood'.

Every now and again.

For a fraction of a second we luck out on an 'aha!' moment.

Something understood.

Even if it remains something we can't explain.

Most faiths involve prayer and while some, like Buddhism, don't rely on a god, the discipline of 'mindfulness' offers its own form of 'prayer'.

Prayer is tuning in.

Opening ourselves to hearing 'the tune which all things hear', to use another of Herbert's hints. It's about joining a conversation with whatever or whoever may be within, behind or beyond it all. It's about another way of being.

Herbert calls it: 'The soul in paraphrase.'

You can kneel, sit in the lotus position, prostrate yourself, go for a stroll.

You can breathe, chant, mutter, shout, say nothing.

You can flatter, beg, reason, provide a shopping list, empty yourself.

You can use a prayer book, repeat a mantra, make it up as you go along, live it out.

You can write to God, speak to the trees, petition the dead, talk to yourself.

You can pray deliberately or allow it to happen.

You can be by yourself or with others.

It doesn't matter how you pray, says the novelist Anne Lamott: 'With your head bowed in silence, or crying out in grief, or dancing'. 'Churches are good for prayer,' she says, 'but so are garages and cars and mountains and showers and dance floors.'

Prayer is not about cause and effect. Or at least not in any way that anyone has ever convincingly explained. It may be about longing or listening. It may be about dreaming or grieving. It may be about changing the world but it is always about changing ourselves.

There is only one rule, says poet Ann Lewin. The rule of waiting. Imagine you want to see a kingfisher. Put yourself where he is likely to be and … wait. Maybe, just when you're about to give up, there it is: '… a flash of brightness/Gives encouragement.'

Something understood.

LIKE JESUS

There's a lot about Jesus that would be useful to know which the Bible doesn't mention. Was he short or tall? Fat or slim? Introvert or extrovert? What did he smell like?

The Bible offers four versions of his life, often known as Gospels: Matthew, Mark, Luke and John. They're not biographies but they drop biographical hints. He came from Nazareth, a village about seventy miles east of Lake Tiberias in the region of Palestine, where it can get quite hot. He ate fish, bread, herbs and lamb. He drank wine. So, he probably smelt of sweat, dust, red wine, and a hint of garlic. Except on that day when his friend Mary Magdalene (possibly) tipped a jar of spikenard on him at a dinner party. That would have added a leathery, aromatic aroma.

People of faith tend to see Jesus as an icon, not as a person. They put 'Lord' before his name and 'Christ' after it, and follow it with phrases like 'King of Kings', or 'Lamb of God'.

In Monty Python's *Life of Brian*, Jesus's – sorry, Brian's – mum tells a crowd of wannabe disciples outside the house: 'He's not the Messiah, he's a very naughty boy.'

There aren't enough stories about his upbringing to know whether he was naughty or not, but on the basis that all children are naughty sometimes, Jesus was no saint. He had brothers: James, Joseph, Judas (not that one) and Simon. He had sisters, one of whom may have been called Salome. Although, while he was alive, none of his siblings 'got him' enough to become followers. At one point, it was family members who 'went out to restrain him, for people were saying: "He's gone out of his mind."' Although … that might have been a drunkle at a wedding.

Maybe his sense of having a special calling rendered him a bit of an outsider. He could be cranky, severe, demanding, infuriating.

But also full of love and compassion; an includer, a champion of the outcast.

Sometimes Jesus of Nazareth appeared driven and conflicted, sure of himself one moment, plagued by self-doubt the next. He was capable of elation and despair. He got tired, lonely. Horny too, no doubt, although we don't know if he was gay or straight.

Churches often teach that Jesus came to show us how to be divine, but probably he came to show us how to be human. To reveal the sacred depths within our humanity. To bring us back from the dead.

Sometimes, from those gospel accounts, he sounds like he could be the person who's best left alone until after the first coffee of the morning. If he said he was off to the hills for some quiet, best not to ask to tag along. And when he went off on one, best not to suggest that he 'calm down'.

On the other hand, if you were a small child; if your world seemed to be falling apart; if you were being bullied by the authorities; if you were at death's door; if you wanted to know you were loved. Jesus was who you'd make for.

In the end, people seemed to know they could trust him. The earth he walked, the divine connection he seemed to have, the people he loved, it all rubbed off on him. You could smell it a mile off.

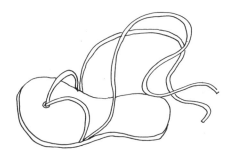

THE VALUE OF NOTHING

The print run of the IKEA catalogue is twice that of the Bible. Furniture is more popular than faith. And often more functional. But there is the odd overlap in the Venn diagram of holy writ and home improvements.

When the sustainability manager of the Swedish superstore announced that the world may have finally reached 'peak stuff', they were cottoning on to something Nazareth's most famous carpenter spoke about: 'For what shall it profit someone if he gains the whole world yet loses his own soul?'

In the world's richest countries, most of us have a lot of stuff. We like to get things. To own, keep and upgrade them. It takes a wise person to know when they have enough.

Some of our stuff is prized for different reasons:

That dog-eared ticket stub from a night we'll never forget.

The car we could never afford. But did.

The ring that once belonged to a lost relative.

We treasure them. Yes. For what they're worth? No.

A cynic, said an Oscar Wilde character, 'knows the price of everything, and the value of nothing'.

It's impossible to price things that can't be bought or sold. The preciousness of some objects doesn't reside in their quality as objects. It's not their *thing*ness that enchants us. It's something less tangible – memory, journey, association.

Writer Art Buchwald summed it up: 'The best things in life aren't things.'

In the end what we value aren't possessions at all. They're things we can never actually own:

The trust of a good friend.
A child's look of amazement.
A first, hesitant kiss.
Finally understanding something.
Knowing we're forgiven.
The kindness of a stranger.

What we hold on to is not what we can hold. What we carry close are priceless imponderables, like love, joy, beauty, friendship and knowledge.

Bean grinder or fancy cappuccino machine? Who cares, if we never wake up and smell the coffee.

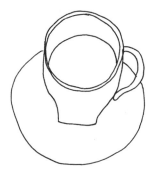

GET LOST IN MUSIC

The screwdriver has not yet been invented which can unscrew the inscrutable. Some things are indescribable. Some days words are the best help we can find. Other days, we need something else.

Something like music.

A tune carries freight. 'Music,' said composer Leonard Bernstein, 'can name the unnameable and communicate the unknowable.'

Talking about three of the greats in classical music, Douglas Adams put it like this: 'Beethoven tells you what it's like to be Beethoven and Mozart tells you what it's like to be human. Bach tells you what it's like to be the universe.'

Music can tell you things by taking you places. It can transport you to heaven, whether you believe in heaven or not. David Bowie suggested that searching for music was like searching for God: 'They're very similar. There's an effort to reclaim the unsayable, the unmentionable, the unseeable, the unspeakable. All of these things come into being for a composer, a writer.'

For instance, when we hear – or *feel* – those left-hand piano chords in Gospel music, our faith is more likely to be stirred than by reciting a shrink-wrapped creed in a religious service. Take that mystical meld of Gospel and rhythm and blues that we call Soul – its visceral rhythm hauls you to your feet, and drives you to the dance floor.

It's body *and* spirit.

Or the act of singing, how you can lose yourself in the melody, how the words no longer matter, how it's subsumed into a feeling of connection. 'Singing,' said Joseph Shabalala of South Africa's Ladysmith Black Mambazo, 'is just like kneeling down and praying.'

Over the centuries, religious institutions have become obsessed with words, attempting to tie down the mystery of existence in polysyllables. Why try so hard when polyphony – that densely woven texture of voice and instrument – does a much better job of embodying that *mysterium tremendum*.

Like Mavis Staples puts it, 'The devil ain't got no music. All music is God's music.'

When you hear a piano playing, especially those sad, indigo-blue phrases that come from the heart of the Mississippi Delta, or when a choral bass drone rolls around the barrel vault of a church, that's the kind of sonic landscape where you can begin to believe that God is in the house.

REMEMBER YOU ARE DUST

We're physical creatures in a physical universe. We're made of matter but not mere material. We are also mind and soul and spirit … and we are bodies, on earth.

Earth.

The word is rich, crumbly, fertile, organic, alive. It's solid, dependable, firm, foundational, nutritional. You can grow in earth, build with it, shape it and fire it, tunnel through it, hollow it out. The earth is our home: we are earthy, grounded, rooted people.

This makes our bodies significant. They will not be dismissed as temporary shells for the soul to travel in, as if the soul or spirit was the real thing and the body simply packaging. There's an inclination, says the psychologist Guy Claxton, in *The Wayward Mind*, to think of our souls as a buried scrap of divinity, 'the immaculate memento of [God's] glory, which [he has] hidden in every human heart'.

The soul or spirit can't be divorced from the rest of who we are. What we are is who we are. In some way we are joined with the air we breathe, the food we eat, the culture that nurtures us, the families who raise us and – some would say – the divinity within us.

Our identities are embodied, embedded, incarnated. It is because we are earthed that place, genes, family, ethnicity, nation, culture and friendship are elemental to us.

We are each and together an ineffable bundle of feeling and thinking, of urges and instinct, of appetite and emotion and gut instinct … which defy reason. We are mysterious moving receivers responding to myriad stimuli in the cycles and rhythms of nature. We are in tune with something we know we don't know.

The poet Wordsworth understood this:

A presence that disturbs me with the joy
Of elevated thoughts; a sense sublime
Of something far more deeply interfused …

A motion and a spirit, that impels
All thinking things, all objects of all thought,
And rolls through all things.

Maybe the earth has soul too. Perhaps the wind and rain, the moon and sun are closer than we know. In which case we might remember, as Christians recite in the liturgy of Ash Wednesday: 'You are dust, and to dust you shall return' …

If soul, spirit, mind, body and earth are so entangled, why the distinction between flesh and spirit, between secular and sacred?

Being alive is to transcend those boundaries.

EVERYBODY HURTS

Shit happens.

It's like gravity, or the second law of thermodynamics.

It affects us all. We can't escape pain and misfortune.

Broken heart or broken leg. Either way, we suffer.

We may get hurt because of something we've done, deliberately, or by accident. Or it may be someone else's doing, on purpose or by mishap. Or it may be no one's doing.

Shit might just happen, through earthquake or illness, through being in the wrong place at the wrong time.

Who's to blame? God? Fate? The alignment of the planets? The government? Our pain may have a cause that we can point to, and even someone who is culpable. But that cause is not the reason for our hurt. Philosophers have tried to find a reason why we suffer. But no one seems to have got much beyond the conclusion that shit happens, and it's random. Bad luck.

In Buddhism, life *is* suffering.

Take up your cross, says Jesus of Nazareth.

Pain and loss mark all our lives and with no evident rhyme or reason. To believe in some all-knowing, all-powerful cosmic project manager – who marks individual pain and pleasure on some universal spreadsheet – is to be stuck with a monstrous divinity of epic proportions. And to cast ourselves as puppets, dancing on strings to a tortured, gothic tune.

Is there another way of looking at this? Alfred North Whitehead, the twentieth-century English mathematician and philosopher, talked instead of a 'fluent' God who joins with us in the process of life. God, he said, is our 'great companion – the fellow-sufferer who understands'.

Someone, as the Hebrew prophet Isaiah put it, who joins in 'bearing our griefs and carrying our sorrows'.

The rock singer Nick Cave, who experienced the loss of his teenage son, was asked if there is any 'utility' in suffering. 'By understanding that suffering is the universal unifying force,' he replied, 'we can see people more compassionately, and this goes some way toward helping us forgive the world and ourselves. By acting compassionately, we reduce the world's net suffering, and defiantly rehabilitate the world.' This he called 'an alchemical act that transforms pain into beauty'. The 'utility of suffering' is in the opportunity to become better human beings, Cave says. It is 'the engine of our redemption'.

And while shit is not meant to happen and bad things are not good, we are not alone. Remarkably, people can emerge bruised but still strong, from a great wreckage which is not of their own making.

In the support of friends and dear ones, in the kindness of strangers, sometimes we may even recognise the presence of some loving companion.

'Everybody hurts' sing REM.

You are not alone.

Hold on.

MAKE A HABIT OF IT

It's Sunday morning, and some ancient programming hardwired deep inside tells someone to go to church.

Perhaps it would be a big decision if they decided *not* to do it, but in recent decades millions of people have made just that decision. They have reprogrammed themselves. They enjoy a divine lie-in; they drink coffee and read the paper, catch up on their social media, call relatives, go to the supermarket, hang out.

In the UK the numbers participating in institutional religion are steadily falling. No religion is becoming the new religion.

But still, around the world, a lot of people continue to wear the religious habit. In Kampala and Manila, in Buenos Aires, Bethlehem and Ho Chi Minh City … on Sundays, people do church.

On Friday, Muslims kneel in prayer at the mosque.

On Saturday, Jews walk to synagogue.

It's ritual. It's habit.

Our habits shape our lives. And good habits are a good habit. When life gets tough, they can help us find hope. 'Hope begins in the dark,' writes Anne Lamott. 'The stubborn hope that if you just show up and try to do the right thing, the dawn will come.'

Any healthy life needs good habits, and in religion, habit is often called ritual. Like other daily habits – cleaning our teeth in the bathroom – once we're in the place of worship, the programming takes over.

Christians, for example, sing songs, make a confession, receive bread and wine, say prayers, give money away, listen to a talk, wonder what it's about, hope it will soon be over. Many have undergone rituals called baptism, or confirmation – public commitments that they will try to follow the way of Jesus of Nazareth.

It's more about behaviour than belief says Karen Armstrong: 'Religion is not about accepting 20 impossible propositions before breakfast, but about doing things that change you. It is a moral aesthetic, an ethical alchemy. If you behave in a certain way, you will be transformed.'

Some rituals we adopt after deliberation, and some we do automatically, without thinking. But all of them contribute to the kind of people we want to be. Our habits inform how we live, without us realising it.

Rituals can be a performance that needs no explaining. Like a mantra, the repetition itself is the meaning. 'Ritual is poetry in action,' said Rabbi Chaim Stern.

The best kind of rituals are a really good habit. The philosopher Aristotle nailed it: 'We are what we repeatedly do. Excellence is not an act, but a habit.'

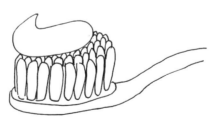

DON'T PUT A PRICE ON IT

No one knows for sure if Leonardo da Vinci painted *Salvator Mundi*, and when it was first 'discovered' in 1958 it was sold for $200 (£145). Nearly sixty years later, after restoration, the painting came on the market again. It sold for $450 million (£327.5 million), the most expensive work of art in history at the time.

In a market economy, supply and demand are in charge. There are barely twenty works by da Vinci in existence, so if one comes on the market demand is stratospheric. But what else could you do with $450 million?

'Drawing is based upon perspective,' said Leonardo, also a brilliant mathematician, 'which is nothing else than a thorough knowledge of the function of the eye.'

Today, medical technology gives us a still more thorough knowledge of how our eyes function. And how they don't if you are one of the 36 million people in the world who are blind. Or one of 200 million with visual impairments, including cataracts, which can be treated with surgery for as little as £24 per person.

You can buy da Vinci's *Salvator Mundi* for $450 million, or you can use that sum to restore sight to 14 million people with cataracts. What will you do?

Living and breathing inside a market economy, we absorb its language and assumptions. We think about how 'hard' we can make our money work or the best return on our investment. But among the downsides of market capitalism is how it persuades us to quantify everything. To price things that are priceless.

How do you value a work of art? Or a friendship? Or public service? How do you value the time spent stopping to talk with a neighbour, or volunteering on a school trip?

Cultural critic Lewis Hyde explored this question in *The Gift*, pointing out that art and creativity often don't fit the world of market forces. Sometimes, he writes, it's better to see life as simply a gift. He cites the 'gift exchange' culture of some ancient societies, where it was understood that everyone participates in a cycle of giving, and the act of giving is an act of faith, a kind of abandonment. You cannot control the 'returns', he says, but it's when a part of the self is given away 'that community appears'.

In a culture where everything has a price tag attached, this seems daft. But life is full of counter-cultural figures who have stepped out of the mainstream to challenge prevailing wisdom. Painters, poets or novelists, for example, who are compelled to follow their art, but whose work may never be acclaimed, and whose books may never be balanced. Nuns or monks who take vows of poverty or chastity, resisting accepted norms in favour of 'unproductive' and inefficient lives.

Sometimes the sensible decision is daft, and the foolish choice is wise. The wisdom of this world, as the first-century Christian teacher Paul put it, may be foolishness.

Someone somewhere has invested $450 million of their money in Leonardo's *Salvator Mundi*. The sensible thing would be to keep it in a safe for a few years before selling it on at a vast profit. But perhaps they'll anonymously donate the painting to a public gallery.

Now, that would be daft.

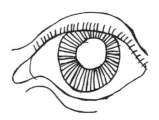

JOIN THE RESISTANCE

A picture was once worth a thousand words, but today maybe it's a photo. An image to transfix the public imagination by capturing, in a single frame, something about the human condition which a library of words can't articulate. Like the quiet resistance of ordinary people.

When in the spring of 2017 a young political activist from Birmingham, Saffiyah Khan, put herself in harm's way to support a woman wearing a hijab who was being menaced by a member of the English Defence League, she had no idea that she was about to experience viral fame.

A photograph of Saffiyah, calm and smiling in the face of a furious male opponent, went around the world. 'You don't scare me,' she seems to be saying, 'I have strength too.' 'Sometimes,' she told reporters later, 'it's more important to smile than to shout.'

The image resonated with that of a young American woman, Iesha L. Evans, standing defiant and alone in the middle of the road, elegant in a long dress, facing down a line of heavily armed riot police at a Black Lives Matters protest in 2016.

Further back too, it recalls a scene in Tiananmen Square in 1989: 'Tank Man', or 'The Unknown Protestor' as he became known, holds a shopping bag in one hand while holding up a formidable force of Chinese tanks with the other.

Images of unlikely daring, even foolishness, of people resisting the presence of a world they do not believe in.

People standing firm whatever the odds.

Captured on film, they draw a fleeting fame; but every day countless others too are resisting the odds – refusing to bow the knee to oppressive governments, or political bullies, or inhuman laws.

Dancing to a different drummer, they constitute a quiet, continuous, disruptive resistance.

An alternative narrative in history.

History sometimes defines people with this kind of counter-cultural fearlessness as heroes. Religions may call them saints: people who choose another way of seeing life. While religions often value saintliness over subversion, true goodness may be less about piety and purity, and more about a defiance which draws on a mysterious inner strength that we may never even know we have.

On 1 December, 1955, a bus driver in Montgomery Alabama demanded that Rosa Parks give up her seat for a white man. Something told Parks she shouldn't. 'When that white driver stepped back toward us, when he waved his hand and ordered us up and out of our seats, I felt a determination cover my body like a quilt on a winter night.'

Arrested and placed in custody Rosa Parks was found guilty in court, but her resistance sparked the Montgomery Bus Boycott and, within a year, the U.S. Supreme Court ruled that bus segregation was unconstitutional.

Sometimes resistance may come with a smile, a subversive twinkle in the eye of an ongoing storm. Walking along a narrow pavement in apartheid South Africa, Desmond Tutu was recognised by a white man who said, 'I don't make way for gorillas.' Tutu made a deep sweeping gesture and said, 'Ah, yes, but I do.'

DUTY CALLS

Growing up most of us had to negotiate a bewildering labyrinth of expectations, often peculiar to our family, school and peer group.

Eat your greens. Don't slam the door. Let Granny give you a kiss. Look at me when I'm talking to you. Throw your litter in the bin. Whatever you do, don't ever call Richard, Dick.

Some were rules, some were for our own good and some were just good manners. But they were all expectations.

Obligations continue into our adult lives and duties and responsibilities multiply … to family, friends, work and our communities. These too often carry the burden of other people's expectations: *'You really ought to …'*

This can breed resentment, a sense of being pushed into a corner. We do our duty, but with bad grace. Or maybe we take our obligations so seriously that we ignore our own wellbeing. We suffer from a 'hardening of the oughteries'.

But we can't live life in isolation. Having family, friends, colleagues and neighbours, means a life of give and take. From taking your turn on the coffee rota or school run to visiting a poorly neighbour or phoning a challenging relative. We're not obliged to do any of this – it's not exactly our duty. But if we don't, then our humanity shrinks a little, we lose touch or feel lonely. Humanity is diminished in some way that's both obvious and immeasurable.

Institutions and organisations are often taken to task about their 'duty of care'. Ultimately, care is at the very heart of obligation. The novelist Albert Camus put it like this: 'I only know of one duty, and that is to love.'

And maybe if we try to love people first, then liking them and doing our duty to them comes easier. That's what the Trappist monk Thomas

Merton figured: 'If we wait for some people to become agreeable or attractive before we begin to love them, we will never begin.' Offering a cold, impersonal 'charity' is just a matter of obligation, he says. It's got little to do with sympathy or understanding.

Obligation isn't a one-way street. At best, our responsibilities spring from mutuality – rooted in the reality of living cheek by jowl with other people. In the old story of Cain and Abel, Cain is asked the whereabouts of his missing brother – the one he'd murdered.

Guilty, and cornered, he retorts: 'Am I my brother's keeper?'

The answer is 'Yes'.

An old way of expressing our thanks was to say, 'much obliged'. Or, to put it another way: 'I owe you one.'

We don't, of course. Not exactly.

But then again, we do.

GOD IS NOT A CHRISTIAN
(or Muslim, or Jew, or Buddhist, or Sikh, or Hindu, or agnostic, or atheist ...)

The Hebrew scriptures came up with the idea that women and men are some kind of copy of the divine. 'So God created man in his own image,' reads the seventeenth-century King James edition of the Bible. 'Male and female created he them ...'

But throughout history we've tended to create God in *our* image. And without anthropomorphic language, how could we picture the divine? A popular childhood version depicts an elderly bearded divinity balancing on a cloud.

We forget that what we see depends on where we stand.

The faith we follow is shaped by where we happened to have grown up. Rosa, born in Italy and raised Catholic, would probably have been Muslim if she'd been born in Pakistan. Akio, raised by his Japanese family in devotion to the invisible spiritual beings of Shinto, would have been Hindu if he'd been born in India.

We are suspicious of the faith stories of others and view doubt as a kind of defeat. We figure the best way to defend our religious take is to attack that of a rival.

But our perspective depends on the angle of our view. 'God is like a mirror,' said Rabbi Harold S. Kushner. 'The mirror never changes, but everybody who looks at it sees something different.'

Sure, there's convergence on the mysteries of prayer and meditation but on other questions different faiths take different views.

They make exclusive truth claims, dismiss those of 'rival' traditions and claim their club has the monopoly on truth.

They specify more and more of the detail, departing the poetics of faith for the prose of the examination set-text.

Faith is forcibly evacuated from the right side of the brain and forced into occupying the left side.

If in doubt, make a creed. Get people to sign up.

But perhaps we don't need to be quite so precise. And saying less can say more. Sympathy, empathy, connection between each other and with the divine … this is the bottom line of all religious pursuit, says Richard Rohr.

Depending on where we start, the satnav might suggest a different route but the destination of faith is shared.

'The goal is always union with the divine.'

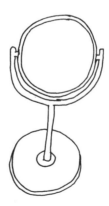

IF IN DOUBT …

Faith is often misunderstood.

The word can echo with certitude, belief, conviction.

But for many people faith is much more fragile.

It's often said that the opposite of faith is doubt.

Maybe not.

'The opposite of faith is not doubt, but certainty,' says Richard Holloway, one time Bishop of Edinburgh, adding that certainty removes the need for faith.

Faith comes into its own precisely when you can't be sure. When you put your life in the hands of a surgeon, for example. A good outcome is statistically probable, but not certain. There's even less verifiable data to rely on when it comes to asking why there's something rather than nothing, or whether there's some presence behind or within, or beyond what we can physically see.

Faith is an experiment, a wager.

Holloway says: 'Faith, by definition, always implies doubt.'

Unlike certainty.

Certainty is cut and dried, black and white.

The poet John Keats believed that doubt was a virtue. He called it 'negative capability'. He was talking about artists who pursue beauty even if it ultimately led them to intellectual confusion or uncertainty. Someone demonstrated such negative capability when they were 'capable of being in uncertainty, mystery, doubt, without irritably reaching after fact or reason'.

Our doubts may be as vital as our faith. The writer Frederick Buechner described doubts as the 'ants in the pants of faith', keeping it awake and moving.

One reason to befriend doubt and uncertainty is that a discomfort with the unprovable may give rise to dangerous certainties. Institutions, religious or political, want to usher their members into dogma and ideology but uncertainty is faith's healthy, necessary shadow side.

'Faith is not an epidural,' writes academic Brené Brown. 'Faith is a midwife.'

Have faith.

Even in doubt.

HOW AND WHY ARE DIFFERENT QUESTIONS

It started roughly 13.5 billion years ago.

It being the event we call the Big Bang which, from the middle of nowhere, produced our small corner of somewhere.

It being matter.

It being energy, time and space.

It being a story which began with 'In the Beginning', when 'God created the heaven and the earth, and called the light Day, and the darkness Night, and the evening and the morning were the first day.'

Not long after the first day – maybe 300,000 years – the matter and energy became atoms, then molecules. A few billion years later, the physics now having hooked up with the chemistry, along came biology when molecules formed structures called organisms and those, like us, began making structures called cultures.

In time – by now everything is in time – human culture produced history. And her story. And the earliest stories were stories of faith. Stories where people – warming themselves around a fire and gazing into a night sky – recalled the original cracking of a cosmic egg which gave birth to everything; or how heroic figures travelled through distant realms to reach this one; or how a supernatural bird from on high dived into the primordial sea to retrieve the mud which became our Earth; or how the all-powerful Creator invented everything out of nothing in six days and then decided a short lie-down was in order. Once a week for everyone.

'Where did we come from and how?' We used our stories to explain to each other about our place in the cosmological order. In painting and music, in poetry and song, we told each other that our lives have meaning. We updated our stories when we learned new things, as

science disclosed the hidden laws that make life possible, as technology enabled us to thrive, not just survive.

For a long time, faith and science lived happily in the stories, but eventually the gatekeepers of faith began losing sleep over the encroachment of science, which they feared was a danger to faith. And some scientists became a little religious. 'Faith is the great cop-out,' wrote Professor Richard Dawkins, 'the great excuse to evade the need to think and evaluate evidence.'

Others, like Albert Einstein, said we needed both: 'Science without religion is lame; religion without science is blind.'

Maybe science and faith are fellow travellers, who tell different stories because they ask different questions. Science is about explanation and religion is about meaning, was how Rabbi Jonathan Sacks framed it. Science tells us what is. Religion tells us what ought to be. 'Science breaks things down to their component parts. Religion binds people together in relationships of trust. Science describes. Religion beckons, summons, calls.'

BEAR WITNESS

Does a million people on a march make any difference? Does two million?

There are moments in history when we are so incensed at the direction our politicians want to take us in that all we can do is take to the streets. Moments when national leaders act only in national interest, while the challenges of our shared planet can only be faced with global collaboration.

At this point even the politically shy and retiring decide that their only course of action is to hold high a handwritten slogan in the company of fellow discontents:

'I am no longer accepting the things I cannot change.
I am changing the things I cannot accept.'

But how come so many people seem to be protesting the same things after so many years of protesting those things? The climate emergency, institutional racism, LGBT+ rights, gender equality. Critics claim demonstrations are incoherent and naive. Against the patriarchy, in favour of rainbows; against tanks, in favour of flowers. But the patriarchy is resilient. Like racism and homophobia, like hatred of Jews or hatred of Muslims. As one placard put it in 2017: 'I can't believe I still have to protest this fucking shit.'

The sentiment was borrowed from a young black woman protesting racism in 2014, half a century after the dawn of the civil rights movement. Occasionally a great uprising of people power ignites dramatic political change – like the fall of the Berlin Wall. More likely, say the cynics, mass protest movements are just virtue-signalling, a way of saying to like-minded people that you're on their team. When did the Occupy movement achieve the reform of capitalism?

But viewing the efficacy of mass protest in short-term policy shifts is not the only lens to use. Asked how he wished to be remembered, the neurologist Oliver Sacks said he'd like it to be thought that he had listened carefully to what patients and others had told him. To use a biblical term, he said he'd like it to be thought that he 'bore witness'.

Sacks understood the significance of bearing witness to the lives of others, often those ostracised or ignored. The most powerful uprisings of public disquiet or longing for social change are not those which are simply about standing up for people but those which are about standing alongside people. Standing with people when the march is over, people where we live or work.

Elie Wiesel lost his sister and mother in Auschwitz, and his father at Buchenwald. His memoir *Night* is about his first night in a camp, 'those moments that murdered my God and my soul and turned my dreams to ashes for ever'. Wiesel spent much of the rest of his life with Holocaust survivors and came to see his role as that of 'a witness', to guard against history repeating itself: 'To listen to a witness is to become a witness and that consoles us.'

How effective is our protest?

'You may never know what results come of your actions,' said Gandhi, 'but if you do nothing, there will be no results.'

We bear witness by telling another kind of story, says the novelist Arundhati Roy, by imagining another kind of being in the world. With our art and music and literature as well as 'our joy, our brilliance, our sheer relentlessness …'

And with our own stories.

Stories that are different from the ones we're being brainwashed to believe …

'Another world is not only possible, she is on her way. On a quiet day, I can hear her breathing.'

RESERVE YOUR SOUL

'Between consenting adults, in private.' It's the sexual norm for almost every society on earth, and the legal definition in most countries.

It's not the most poetic phrase but, to be fair, it's there for legal clarification, and personal protection. And very reasonable. Trouble is, sex itself is not reasonable at all. It's primal. It's sensual, lustful, passionate and sticky.

Cognitive scientist and psychologist Steven Pinker says that sex and excretion are reminders that any claim we have to 24-hour dignity is pretty tenuous: 'The so-called rational animal has a desperate drive to pair up and moan and writhe.'

If there's a moment when we as humans really let go, it's in the instant of sexual climax. Pure pleasure. Ecstasy. Heaven. That's why the killjoys of religion have tried to put the dampener on it.

And because sex is such a visceral drive – our bodies can easily rule our heads, and hearts – it's readily exploited, commodified. People with influence, or glamour, or money, or guns, can use sex to express their power. Meanwhile, those without may be the victims of that power, driven to sell their bodies to gratify the appetite of others.

For animals, sex is mostly about procreation, though research suggests not in all species. And while making babies is hugely enjoyable for humans, it's about a whole lot more. The powerful urge remains but it's more than about satisfying a physical hunger. It's about coupling – in the most generous sense of the word. It's about touch and heat and smell.

Intimacy.

An eloquence of trust and fidelity.

Our bodies tell each other what we love about them.

Sacred texts are often read to assume that this takes place between one gender and another. The creation myth of the Hebrew and Christian scriptures, for instance, describes the creation of man and woman, saying: 'Therefore shall a man leave his father and his mother, and shall cleave unto his wife and they shall be one flesh.'

Great word, 'cleave'.

Because these texts emerged in a time before we understood the fluidity of gender and identity, the underlying wisdom can be missed. It's the *cleaving* that matters, however we're built.

The seventeenth-century King James Bible says that in having sex with someone, we 'know' them.

'Real intimacy is a sacred experience,' chimes poet John O'Donohue. 'It never exposes its secret trust and belonging to the voyeuristic eye of a neon culture. Real intimacy is of the soul, and the soul is reserved.'

Body and soul, consenting, in private.

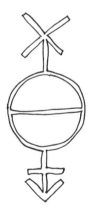

FIND A WAY HOME

Exile is a brutal reality for increasing numbers of displaced people. But it's more than geographical. It's possible to be an exile in your homeland, in your own house.

Politics, persecution or conflict drives many into foreign exile, and while they accommodate to their new surroundings, at heart there remains a painful sense of homelessness.

For some exiled communities this is expressed in a nostalgia for language, food, objects or traditions, which provide comfort and bolster their sense of identity.

But exile can be as much about the mind or spirit as about physical location. Minorities – for example, people with disabilities, individuals in the LGBT+ community, people of colour – often feel marginalised and disadvantaged in the very communities in which they were born and raised. Alienated in their own country.

And we are increasingly strangers to the land itself. Often, our buildings and towns are designed as a way of exiling us from nature: defending ourselves from its invasion.

But exile need not necessarily be terminal. At the turn of the fourth and fifth century BC, Nebuchadnezzar destroyed Jerusalem, and condemned most Israelites to exile in Babylon. The darkest of days. They had thought they had a divine guarantee of protection and prosperity. But exile wasn't the end, it didn't lead the people to abandon their faith or sink into despair. On the contrary, as the Old Testament scholar Walter Brueggemann observed, it 'evoked the most brilliant literature … It was during the exile that they gathered their scriptures, their traditions and culture around them. And dared to hope.'

Palestinian, Muslim poet Mahmoud Darwish, no stranger to exile, responded in a similar way. 'I've built my homeland, I've even founded my own state – in my language.'

And, like exiles across history and around the world, he held on and made plans for a return home. 'We suffer from an incurable malady,' he said: 'Hope.'

Whenever, however, we're exiled, we need to find our way home.

EXPECT THE UNEXPECTED

'Do you believe in God?' The question defies an easy answer, because the person asking the question and the person invited to answer may be talking about something different.

God is beyond definition.

By definition.

God is not a fact, or a thing.

But sometimes gives herself up.

Like someone who coughs while hiding. As the German mystic Meister Eckhart put it in the fourteenth century: 'God lies in wait for us with nothing so much as love.'

He understood that the best way to approach the idea of God is in metaphor.

The most famous poem in the Bible, the 23rd Psalm, begins: 'The Lord is my shepherd ...' God is the shepherd and people are the sheep. David, if he was the author, had been a shepherd himself once and comes up with a picture of divine protection true to life. But more true in an ancient agrarian culture than in a twenty-first-century, urban metropolis.

Sacred texts are big on metaphor. In the Hebrew Bible God is described as a father, a burning bush, a whisper, a judge and a chicken. And, since human lives are essentially story-shaped, the scriptures also go big on narrative. The stories told by people of faith are an attempt to bring their out-of-the-ordinary experiences down to earth. But still, God seems elusive, shy, speedy even.

One ancient tradition, the *via negativa*, suggests that the presence of the divine is discovered in its apparent absence. The poet and priest R.S. Thomas said in that great absence is where we go seeking.

Maybe that's what critic George Steiner was reaching for when he wrote of 'a nearness out of reach, of a remembrance torn at the edges'·

Was that a cough?

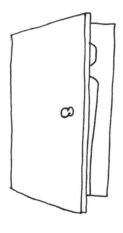

DISORIENTATE YOURSELF

By the rivers of Babylon,
there we sat down, yea, we wept,
when we remembered Zion.

We hanged our harps upon the willows in the midst thereof
for there they that carried us away captive
required of us a song;
and they that wasted us required of us mirth,
saying, Sing us one of the songs of Zion.
How shall we sing the Lord's song in a strange land?

The words of a disco banger from Boney M?

Wrong.

And also right.

The words come originally from Psalm 137, part of a collection of 150 ancient poems sometimes called the Psalter and among the most beautiful of the Hebrew and Christian scriptures. It was Boney M, in the 1970s, who popularised a reggae song by The Melodians, 'Rivers of Babylon', that had drawn on the psalm. It's a lament of those Jews exiled from the land of their birth after the Babylonians took their capital Jerusalem, some six centuries before the birth of Jesus.

The Psalms are among those ancient sacred writings which refresh themselves in every generation. For example, the rebirth of the psalm as a reggae number had special resonance for Rastafarians, for whom the word 'Babylon' had come to suggest any oppressive regime. This venerable collection of poetry captures common human experience, from fear to ecstasy, from despair to joy.

But nor do they flinch from the most base human instincts, as the singer Nick Cave observed, reflecting on how they had inspired his songwriting: 'I found the Psalms, which deal directly with the relationship between man and God, teeming with all the clamorous desperation, longing, exaltation, erotic violence and brutality that I could hope for.'

If the Psalms have inspired gospel songs and hymns, perhaps, suggests another singer, they're even more influential in the story of the blues. Here's how Bono puts it:

'That's what a lot of the psalms feel like to me, the blues. Man shouting at God: "My God, my God, why hast thou forsaken me? Why art thou so far from helping me?" (Psalm 22). The Psalter may be a font of gospel music, but for me it's despair that the psalmist really reveals and the nature of that special relationship with God. Honesty, even to the point of anger. "How long, Lord? Wilt thou hide thyself forever?" (Psalm 89), or "Answer me when I call" (Psalm 5).'

Leonard Cohen, Mavis Staples, Jessi Colter, Bob Dylan, Paul Simon ... countless artists find inspiration in the Psalms and have taken to writing their own.

A Psalm, says Bible scholar Walter Brueggemann, may do one of three things to a reader:

Sometimes a psalm will orientate you – remind you where you're going. Sometimes it will disorientate you – turn you upside down. Sometimes it will completely re-orientate you. That's when it gives us another way of seeing, suggests another road to take.

'Though I walk through the valley of the shadow of death, I will fear no evil: for thou art with me; thy rod and thy staff they comfort me.'

CELEBRATE RELIGION

'That's me in the corner … losing my religion.'

An unlikely theme for an unlikely song, REM's 1991 hit 'Losing My Religion' is actually a play on a popular southern U.S. expression for losing your cool.

It could as easily be an anthem for an entire movement. People who actually were losing their faith – or at least coming clean that they didn't have one.

'We're not here to tell you how to live your life,' reads the charter of Sunday Assembly. 'We're here to help you be the best version of you you can be.'

A secular congregation that 'celebrates life', Sunday Assembly is a religious group which … isn't religious. It was founded by a couple of comedians, Sanderson Jones and Pippa Evans, who wanted to do something that was like church but entirely secular and inclusive. It has no doctrine ('We have no set texts so we can make use of wisdom from all sources'), and no deity ('We don't do supernatural but we also won't tell you you're wrong if you do').

Professor Linda Woodhead of Lancaster University says that more people in Britain now say they have no religion (46 per cent) than identify with Christianity (44 per cent). She calls them the 'nones', and says 'no religion is the new norm'. The 'nones', she says, aren't hostile to faith, it just doesn't do it for them.

Many people who've come to believe life can make sense without a deity, have also decided they don't need to waste energy in attacking those who do do God. Far from attacking religion, says philosopher Alain de Botton, agnostics and atheists should be plundering it. Instead of lamenting how it's scientifically implausible they should celebrate how it's psychologically helpful. Faith traditions are ripe with resources for living and organising society, bursting with insight into how to build community, strengthen relationships, appreciate art and overcome our feelings of inadequacy.

Even if you've lost your religion.

What religion has discovered must be decoupled from its supernatural moorings so that everyone else can use it to stay afloat on life's choppy waters. 'The wisdom of the faiths,' de Botton writes in *Religion for Atheists*, 'belongs to all of mankind, even the most rational among us, and deserves to be selectively reabsorbed by the supernatural's greatest enemies.'

LISTEN TO THE SILENCE

'All men's miseries derive from not being able to sit quietly in a room alone.'

And if Blaise Pascal, seventeenth-century French philosopher and misery guts had lived today, he would doubtless have included women too.

But was he onto something?

In an experiment reported in the journal *Science*, researchers at the University of Virginia invited forty people to sit alone in an empty room for twenty minutes. No electronic gadgets allowed, not even a watch.

A button, if pressed, would let them exit the room, but would also give them an electrical shock. Everyone gave it a practice press, received a practice shock and vowed they'd pay money to avoid receiving that shock again.

Then they were asked to sit still with their own thoughts and not fall asleep. Most people reported how difficult it was, even unpleasant. Just sitting there, doing nothing. Two-thirds of the men and a quarter of the women found their own company so troubling that they chose the electric shock treatment.

We want stimulation.

We long to be needed.

Perhaps this is the 'age of distraction' because we like it that way. We're unsure of what we might find if we turned inward, instead of always outward. Perhaps we confuse being alone with being lonely.

We might be mistaken.

An intentional solitude can be like a wakeful sleep. Just as sleep helps the mind to process and organise the chaos of thought – so that sometimes we wake up with a clarity we couldn't find before – so sitting alone in quiet, determining to resist the distractions, can be regenerative.

It can renew our friendship with our own selves. It can orientate us by locating us. It can calm us.

There is nothing to fear in choosing a period of solitude. At the kitchen table, with the radio turned off. In the bedroom, when everyone else has left the flat, smartphone exiled. A lunchtime walk from the office, turning through the doors of that building we rarely look twice at.

Michael Palin, former Monty Python member, recalls taking a lunch break after being cross-questioned in a court case in London. Not permitted to talk to anyone, he wanted somewhere to sit quietly and get himself together. Unable to find a seat which didn't involve eating, drinking or some commercial transaction, he stumbled upon the Church of St Dunstan-in-the-West in the heart of Fleet Street. 'I was never so grateful for a place of repose, an oasis of peace and quiet in the midst of the mayhem,' he said.

In the furious activity of a world where the volume is turned up, houses of worship may be just the place to sit quietly and alone, to hear the silence speak.

'Churches are vessels of hush, as well as everything else they are,' says novelist Francis Spufford. 'And when I block out the distractions of vision, the silence is almost shockingly loud.'

THIS SITUATION SHALL PASS ...

A famous entertainer endures the final days of illness: she's 'in our thoughts and prayers'. A family we know face tragedy: 'Our thoughts and prayers are with them.' Innocent civilians, caught in a war zone: 'They're in our thoughts and prayers.'

It's the catch-all, go-to phrase for public figures who rarely draw on the vocabulary of faith. A politician, for example, puts 'thoughts' in front of 'prayers' to moderate the religious aspect. They want to convey empathy without pretending that they – or we – are as devout as we once were.

Sometimes the 'prayer' word is dropped completely. Sending 'all strength, thoughts and best wishes'. It's the thought that counts, even when our words can feel like they don't count for much. If we can't honestly pray for someone, we can let them know we're thinking well of them.

The roots of the phrase 'thoughts and prayers' go back to 1821, and the *Christian Herald and Seaman's Magazine*, sadly no longer on sale. 'Masters and seamen,' writes the author, 'as you are about to leave us for the season, I trust we shall follow you in our thoughts and prayers.' Doubtless they did, and the expression had more than sea legs.

Finding the right words is tricky in an age of religious diversity – acknowledging the possibility of faith without alienating those who don't share it.

All of us do thoughts, but we don't all do prayer. At least not in the way people have often thought of prayer, as communication with an unseen power in a manner which transforms our experience of life. But there is a kind of prayer that doesn't ask whether or not God exists, but understands that contemplation and reflection are in themselves transformative.

The twentieth-century French painter Henri Matisse wasn't sure if he believed in God, but late in life he designed a small chapel for the Dominican Sisters in the town of Vence on the French Riviera. He said: 'I don't know whether I believe in God or not. But the essential thing is to put oneself in a frame of mind which is close to that of prayer.'

Sometimes we overrate belief and underplay experience, but the practice of prayer can transcend any creed. On those days when we can't find the words for what is happening in our lives or in our world, maybe all we can do is:

Light a solitary candle on the kitchen table.
Stand without words in a two-minute silence.
Lay a flower at the roadside.
Bow in respect as the funeral cortège goes by.

Sometimes a prayer is as simple as this poem, by Michael Leunig:
'These circumstances will change. This situation shall pass. Amen.'

MAKE A NEST

'Why do you wear that cross round your neck?'

The answer may be different every time it's asked. As it would if it were asked of people wearing a hijab, or a yarmulke.

These physical markers are signs of something which is usually invisible. But like tattoos, tribal scars and badges they have a symbolic power, saying something about our spiritual, emotional or political allegiances. But not saying everything.

And the meaning may shift, depending on whether someone wants to stand out … or fit in. A Muslim may describe her hijab as a signal that she is not owned by society, that her ultimate allegiance lies elsewhere.

These signatures go beyond religion.

We have a kind of nesting instinct to populate our lives with signs and markers of what we value. We treasure photographs of loved ones, together with mementos of memorable experiences: a pebble carried home from a beach, a kitsch souvenir from a holiday resort. Hanging on a wall or sitting on a mantelpiece, they're domestic versions of prayer shrines with their icons and candles. We make our nests mobile – carrying around familiar emblems in our wallets, purses and phones.

When someone we love dies, we're faced with the clearance of their belongings and some heart-rending decisions. What to sell, what to give away, what to junk and what to keep. The mementos we decide to hold on to may have no financial value, but they're rich in meaning and memory. A brooch, scarf, book or pipe which is redolent with personal history. These objects are significant – physical bulwarks against forgetting.

They give a kind of life back to someone who has died.

They keep them alive in our hearts.

They make the invisible visible.

This investment in symbols is deeper than we may know. The things we wear, the objects we hold dear, and the tokens we treat as sacred are part of our identity. They reassure us of who we are, and connect us to worlds beyond the immediate.

They are post-it notes which remind us of the invisible threads of relationship and values that hold our lives together.

Rooted in tradition or in history they are not merely about the past.

They help us negotiate the here and now.

They are signs of life.

GAZE AT THE BEAUTY

'Gaze at the beauty of the green earth,' said the philosopher and mystic Hildegard of Bingen 900 years ago. 'Now think …'

We've been thinking ever since and, somewhere between then and now, some of our thoughts became dangerous. We began to think of Earth as a resource. A tank to drain, a forest to raze, a home to ransack.

But Hildegard was suggesting a contrary notion, the kind that Francis of Assisi had a century or so later, when he talked of Brother Sun and Sister Moon, when he mused on Sister Water, Brothers Wind and Air. Of Mother Earth.

Francis wasn't thinking of Earth as a resource but as a relative. If that thought might have been unremarkable in earlier, aboriginal cultures, today it's been marginalised. We've moved from a relational view of this universe to an instrumental view. From Earth as holy ground to building site. From ecstatic to extractive.

Perhaps population movements to the city accelerated this, obscuring our experience of the shifting seasons captured in fields and trees: shrinking our sense of how we all spring from this earth and autumn into it. The interdependence between us and this earth. How all of life connects.

Thinking this through, Buddhist monk Thich Nhat Hanh coined the word 'interbeing' to capture the interconnectedness of everything. How this planet is a living, breathing cell. How we do not live *in* nature but *are* nature.

Sister Dorothy Stang moved from the U.S. to live among the poorest people in Brazil's Amazon Basin. She ran schools and studied Brazilian law, as a way of supporting local forest dwellers in their stand against corporations exploiting the Amazon.

Wearing a T-shirt which read 'The death of the forest is the end of our lives,' Dot wouldn't be silenced even in the face of death threats. Local farmers, she said, want to 'live and work with dignity while respecting the environment'.

In February 2005, when she was walking alone in the jungle, two gunmen came out of the bushes. Opening her Bible, she started reading the Beatitudes to them: 'Blessed are the poor ...' She was shot dead at 73 years of age.

Some people have called Sister Dot the Patron Saint of Extinction Rebellion. At her funeral, a local farmer stood up and said, 'Sister Dot, we are not burying you: we are planting you.'

If we think of Earth as relation, not resource, we think of all life differently.

'Humanity, take a good look at yourself,' said Hildegard way back when. 'Inside, you've got heaven and earth, and all of creation. You're a world – everything is hidden in you.'

'Gaze at the beauty of the green earth. Now think ...'

ONLY REMEMBER

'Fading away like the stars of the morning,
Losing their light in the glorious sun –
Thus would we pass from the earth and its toiling,
Only remembered by what we have done ...'

Every headstone tells a story. A soldier who lost his life in the Great War. A baby buried at three weeks old in the 1850s. A policeman who died 'bravely doing his duty'. The mossy gravestones in urban graveyard or village burial ground are like antique tweets, concise tablets of memory, keeping alive the narrative of history behind bramble and branches. They tell us if war was underway, or an epidemic in full force. If there was civil unrest. How the times were a-changing.

Adjust your vision from the dog walker having a smoke on a bench, look past the leaf-sodden pathways and find a forgotten history, a place where the dead keep our memories. The act of remembering – in a personal calendar, or on a headstone – is time well spent.

Autumn offers a season of remembering, which once had its own chant:

'Remember, remember, the fifth of November ...'

The surface memory may obscure a deeper, more troubling one. If this English folk verse originated in the failure of the Catholic Guy Fawkes' attempt to blow up the Protestant-run Houses of Parliament in 1605, its apparent anti-treason message was often cover for anti-Catholic prejudice.

But Bonfire Night has been the victim of a reverse takeover by Halloween – and the meaning of Halloween has changed too. It was not always about opening the door to seven-year-olds in fright masks. In the

Christian tradition, it begins three days of Hallowmas: All Hallows' Eve (Halloween) followed by All Hallows' Day or All Saints' Day, which is followed by All Souls' Day. The dead are remembered. In some countries they call it the Day of the Dead.

In the same season, on 11 November, at war memorials around Britain people stop still and stand silent on Remembrance Day. The silence speaks sadness but also protest at the way things are. Somewhere underneath, it may also speak of a longing for a different future. Summoning the past into the present we try to remember another future.

A conversation with a First World War veteran who'd worked with horses gave novelist Michael Morpurgo an idea for a story about Joey, a horse purchased by the Army to serve in the war, and how Albert, his previous owner, tried to bring him home.

In the long-running stage play of *War Horse*, one song, 'Only Remembered', haunts the imagination. The song is adapted from Horatius Bonar's nineteenth-century hymn but the original text – in which the faithful believer is rewarded in heaven – can't make the transition to a play about the horror of the Great War.

That said, a common truth binds them: that what we do here and now is how we will be remembered. That who we are now is who we become in the future.

The song remembers the past, but also asks how what we do now will make a difference to those in the future, when we too are the past.

'Only the truth that in life we have spoken,
Only the seed that on earth we have sown;
These shall pass onward when we are forgotten.'

OWN IT, NOTE IT, FIX IT

It's as old as the hills. Even the hills conjured up by the Maker of All Things in the original creation stories.

In the shake of a fig leaf, the story goes, the serpent tempts Eve, who takes a bite from the apple before recommending it to Adam. Now they notice they're buck naked, overcome with shame and the age of innocence is at an end. An ancient reading in misogyny, body image and snakes but also something religions have majored on ever since.

Sin.

Sin is the most popular religious explanation for our existential angst, the separation of creature from Creator. In this paradise we fell into sin. 'We acknowledge and bewail our manifold sins and wickedness,' as it's put in the *Book of Common Prayer* of the Church of England. 'There is no health in us miserable offenders.'

Harsh.

Cast out of our divine home, different faith traditions offer competing routes back. But the lexicon of sin, wickedness and moral depravity is less persuasive than it once was. And definitions of sin honed in on sex, hatred of the body or some combination.

But the idea of 'sin' may not be redundant while it usefully describes a human emotion that rings true. Most of us feel that we mess up. We fail by our own standards, even if we don't believe there are divine standards.

The human species, says novelist Francis Spufford, suffers from 'HPtFTU' – the 'Human Propensity to Fuck Things Up'. That's not just the mayhem we cause by accident or by neglect, but our 'active inclination' to break stuff, including promises, or relationships, or our own wellbeing … as well as the systems and structures that social peace and justice can flourish in.

That seventeenth-century *Book of Common Prayer* may still touch a nerve when it says we have 'erred, and strayed like lost sheep', or 'followed too much the devices and desires of our own hearts'. Most of us have hurt people; been greedy, selfish and proud. It happens. Not just us on our own, but in our families, our communities, our countries.

We have fucked up history.

We fail each other. We fail ourselves.

It's part of the truth about ourselves.

On a good day, we see it and admit it.

We confess it.

Only when we recognise that we fuck things up, and that we're likely to do it again, do we have a chance to do something about it. Not to do it again.

BELIEVE IN LOVE

All of this is less solid and more fluid than we've been often led to … believe.

'I believe', as someone once said to Jesus of Nazareth. 'Help me in my unbelief.'

It's possible to believe and not believe at the same time.

Our beliefs ebb and flow, depending on the terrain life asks us to cross.

We lose someone we love. The work dries up and money runs out. Our anxiety rises in a climate emergency or cost of living crisis. We fall out with someone and don't know how to fall back in. We make mistakes and hold regrets.

Now what do we believe?

In 1563 the Church of England published its *Thirty-nine Articles of Religion*. (For example: 'we confess that vain and rash swearing is forbidden'.) Previously, Thomas Cranmer had come up with 'The Ten Articles' ('The observance of various rites and ceremonies as good and laudable, such as clerical vestments, sprinkling of holy water, bearing of candles on Candlemas-day, giving of ashes on Ash Wednesday …').

Institutional religion goes big on belief … and falls out over it. At a Church version of the European Union, in Nicaea in AD 325, a treaty called the Nicene Creed was settled on. A version of that, the Apostles' Creed, is still recited in many churches, bursting with answers to questions people were asking 1,700 years ago. Questions most of us are no longer asking.

Meantime, the meaning of the word 'belief' has changed. Marcus Borg pointed out that in English, prior to about 1600, the verb 'believe' always had a person as its direct object, not a statement. It did not mean believing a statement is true (say, 'I believe in the Virgin Birth'), but more like what we mean when we say to somebody: 'I believe in you.'

To believe *in* somebody is not the same as believing somebody.

'I believe in you' means having confidence in you – for people of faith that means having confidence in the divine. The old English *be loef* is the root of the word believe and it means 'to hold dear' and is related to the word 'belove'.

The etymology of belief was once about *trust*, but somewhere down the line, the trust element in faith was displaced in favour of the 'mental assertion of an extremely long list of facts' element. In favour of insiders versus outsiders. Those who can sign up to every line of a creed and those who can't.

Actually, said Borg, the Latin root of the word *credo* (from which we get 'creed') means 'I give my heart to'. Heart, he said, is a metaphor for the self at its deepest level: 'a level of the self beneath our thinking, willing and feeling'.

'Do you believe in me?' meant 'Do you belove me?'

In the end beliefs are often overrated.

There is only one article of faith.

Love.

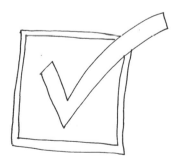

CELEBRATE GOOD TIMES

A mountain of courgettes. A heap of apples. A pile of peas. A hill of beans.

Summer and early autumn are ripe and luscious. In a good year – for even small-scale gardeners – there's too much to consume, which precipitates a flurry of freezing, pickling and preservation.

There's a special delight in having to wait for the season to turn up, watching fruit and veg grow daily more plump and glossy, until that final moment when they're right for the table.

'To everything there is a season', says the ancient author of Ecclesiastes. Her ruminations were turned into a song, 'Turn! Turn! Turn!' by the folk singer Pete Seeger, and then made into a pop hit by the Byrds. There's 'a time to plant, a time to reap', runs Ecclesiastes. 'A time to weep, and a time to laugh; a time to mourn, and a time to dance.'

Harvest is a signal for feasting and festivity, born out of a year's laborious preparation: digging, tilling, feeding, waiting, weeding and protecting.

A celebration is all the sweeter when it comes out of a time of testing. A welcome pint after a hard week, or a decent lie-in after a run of broken nights. They're important tags, a way of saying anything from 'We did it!', to 'Phew, I'm glad that's over!'

Every year, Muslims mark Eid – an eruption of feasting that is anticipated through the thirty days fasting of Ramadan. Jews think carefully about what delicacies they'll consume after the fast of Yom Kippur. For Sikhs, the New Year festival of Baisakhi (or Vaisakhi) originally grew out of the harvest festivities in the Punjab. In the Christian calendar, the Easter festival emerges from the reflective forty days of Lent.

Celebrations – religious or not – are holy. Holidays. They're like book-marks telling us where we've got up to. A way to mark that something significant has been achieved, of saying thank you to friends, family, teammates, the divine … whoever.

In a festive pause, we look one another in the eye, we repeat old stories, we raise a glass, we celebrate the past, and the present, and look to the future. *There's a party going on right here …*

WAIT (WHAT?)

In the year 01999 (1999 to the rest of us) an American foundation bought part of a mountain in eastern Nevada. In this remote area of white limestone cliffs, they planned to build an unusual kind of clock. A clock that ticks just once a year. It would have a century hand not an hour hand, moving only once every hundred years.

The 10,000 Year Clock is the dream of inventor Danny Hillis, who believes in what musician Brian Eno calls 'The Long Now'.

At the Long Now Foundation, they see time differently. They want to signal that life is not about speed but presence, not about faster and cheaper, but slower and deeper. None of them will live to see the hand on the clock move, but that's okay because the 10,000 Year Clock takes the long view.

It's the same perspective as a story told about the fourteenth-century founders of New College Oxford. The college dining hall was made with a series of oak beams across the ceiling, which, half a millennium later, by the end of the nineteenth century, had become infested with beetles. The college called in a man who farmed their land, who responded: 'Ah – we wondered when you might get in touch.' He told them of a tradition going back to the fourteenth century that a grove of oaks had been planted on college land to replace those cut down for the dining-hall beams. These oaks were set aside, and century after century, the farmers had waited.

Today we're less patient.

We like to have things now.

Our deliveries are tracked and we monitor their journeys towards us. We don't wait for the seasons to change before buying particular fruit or veg, because our supermarkets ship them from different seasons across the world.

Waiting feels like time-wasting.

Waiting times are to be reduced.

But sometimes, it's waiting that will tell us what we need. In the calendar of the Christian Church an entire season called Advent is given over to waiting, longing, for a new kind of world to be born.

A time when time will be called on history.

When time will be up.

It's a tradition that grew from the story of the Hebrew people waiting for their Messiah. A waiting which had developed since slavery in Egypt, grown through exile in Babylon, and been incubated under Roman captivity. 'A voice cries out in the wilderness,' said the prophet Isaiah, about 2,700 years ago. 'Prepare the way of the Lord, make straight in the desert a highway.'

It's an active waiting. An alert, vigilant and intentional patience which recognises that we all live in a long now, and that history will not be fast-forwarded.

Like sleep, waiting can't be rushed.

We wait to find out who we are.

Perhaps to discover we are waiting for something we didn't know about.

And we understand what we're here for and what we can do.

Wait.

What?

HEAR THE CALL

You get up in the morning and do what you do.

It's what you always do.

It's become your life.

But something inside you tells you this is not the thing you want to be doing.

It just isn't *you*.

It's not even that it's the wrong thing, just that it's not the right thing.

It's not all of who you are.

Or even most.

'What should I do with my life?' That's the question we ask yourself when that sense of vague unease becomes articulate enough to become a question.

In a survey half of British people said they'd take a pay cut in exchange for a job which gave them a sense of self-worth. Two thirds said they were 'unfulfilled or drifting'.

A vague sense of disappointment with our paid work can hit all of us at different times – and even thinking about options can be seen as a luxury when millions of people toil long hours in field or factory just to put food on the table or a child through school.

But asking what we should do with our lives isn't a question confined to our job. It's about how we're built as people and about how we become ourselves.

At one time this kind of thing was called a vocation – from the Latin *vocare*, meaning 'call'. And if you believed in God, as most people then did, the question was about what God was calling you to do. People had visions and heard voices. The literature of faith is ink-stained with divine messaging which leaves people with little uncertainty about what to do next.

It's all a bit fuzzier for most of us.

Life poses questions to which there aren't always answers. We have to negotiate them daily … or maybe reframe them.

We ask what we're good at, what brings us fulfilment, where we find ourselves and this is how we begin to make ourselves up.

But none of us find this out quickly.

Or finally.

The writer Po Bronson interviewed 900 people who'd switched from one path in life to another: a stockbroker who became a fish farmer; an estate agent who opened a craft factory in Central America; a lawyer who became a priest.

The call, he found, crept up on people, over time, bit by bit. It was usually hedged around with doubt and fear. There was never any writing on the wall, only a feeling in the gut.

'Most of us don't get epiphanies,' says Bronson. 'We only get a whisper – a faint urge.'

The false starts and detours are all part of how we get there, how we become ourselves.

How we hear the call.

GIVE THANKS

When we're young we're taught to say please and thank you.

But as soon as we're old enough to see life is a gift, giving thanks is more than best behaviour.

It's:

How the sun rises again.

Or how that mother cares for her child.

How two strangers meet and find they were made for each other.

A walk by the sea in winter.

Those countries at war, how they made peace.

The roar of the crowd at a match.

A bass riff …

… a bag of chips.

To stop – on the street, in the hallway, during a meal – and notice this one moment. How briefly we are here.

How briefly we are with each other.

This is the moment when we cultivate gratitude in sensing the generosity that surrounds us:

In the people who came before us who made the world we take for granted.

In the invisible people across this world who produce the food and clothes and gadgets we rely on.

In the visible people we work and live with who illuminate our lives with kindness or patience or loyalty or trust.

In our best selves even, how we made it to here … how, some days, we're not so bad after all.

Verbalising gratitude helps embed it in our ways of living. In their later years, the politician Denis Healey and his wife Edna would stroll round their garden and say to one another: 'AWL.' That was their shorthand for 'Aren't We Lucky?'

It was how they reminded each other that they were grateful.

Thanks can even contain a hint of defiance – being grateful for the light in life even when the dark attempts to extinguish it. 'Thank you we are saying and waving dark though it is' is how the poet W.S. Merwin says it.

A dumbstruck glance at the night-time stars.

A grace before a meal.

A folding of the hands.

An inward smile.

The trickling tear at the funeral of a friend.

A muttered prayer that we don't even understand ourselves.

Mediaeval philosopher Meister Eckhart put it like this. 'If the only prayer you ever pray is "thanks", that will be enough.'

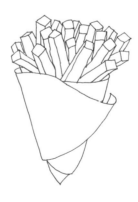

PRACTISE RESURRECTION

It would be good if death was not the end of us. If, when we breathe our last, this veil of tears is drawn back to reveal some beautiful welcome of peace, love and understanding. Death will always ask us to wonder whether our end is *the* end. Witness Shakespeare's Hamlet:

For in that sleep of death what dreams may come
When we have shuffled off this mortal coil, must give us pause.

But none of us know what comes next.

Or even if, after we've identified our coil and shuffled off it, there is a next. Still, we wonder. Maybe harbour longing, for something more.

Perhaps it's simply the rude implausibility of accepting that someone we know so dearly – their looks and ways of speaking, the times we shared, their loves and hates – can simply cease to be.

It's as difficult to believe they're gone as to believe they aren't.

Maybe our instinct is evolutionary, the witness of nature: how every year the life of the earth falls with the seasons into sleep, before rising into life, hungry for the light.

Humans have always cherished notions of a life beyond death. Or of resurrection, returning from death to life. From stories of a deity who dies and rises, to the belief that everyone will be present as history's final credits roll. A reckoning. A Last Judgement. Blinking and rubbing his eyes, say the Christians, Jesus of Nazareth walked out of the tomb on the third day, a promise that 'death has lost its sting'.

Truth be told, death still stings.

Like nothing else.

And, with or without faith, there's no way to be sure, if he did, or didn't. Our certainties are restricted to life before death, which has its own discrete resurrection qualities.

Put your faith in the two inches of humus that will build under the trees every thousand years says farmer-poet Wendell Berry, inviting his readers to 'practise resurrection'. Be joyful, he says, 'though you have considered all the facts'.

Franciscan Richard Rohr says one way to practise resurrection is to practise life now as we would want to practise life in the kind of world we can only dream about. Here's ten of his suggestions:

1. *Refuse to identify with negative, blaming, antagonistic, or fearful thoughts (you cannot stop 'having' them).*
2. *Apologise when you hurt another person or situation.*
3. *Undo your mistakes by some positive action toward the offended person or situation.*
4. *Always seek to change yourself before trying to change others.*
5. *Choose as much as possible to serve rather than be served.*
6. *Whenever possible, seek the common good over your mere private good.*
7. *Give preference to those in pain, excluded, or disabled in any way.*
8. *Seek just systems and policies over mere charity.*
9. *Make sure your medium is the same as your message.*
10. *Never doubt that it is all about love in the end.*

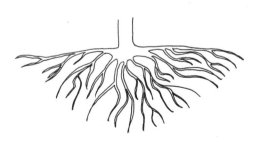

LOVE ACTUALLY

Whatever we believe about religion or faith, most people think that love is a good place to start from, a good place to head to and a good way to get there.

'All you need is love,' we sing.

And we do need it.

Yes. But. What exactly does that mean?

Love is not a thing you can get, or own. And it's more than a feeling you find described in a pop song or a sensation that mysteriously comes and goes.

Love is a verb.

And a verb is a *doing* word.

Love only has real meaning when we demonstrate it. By being loving. Flowers, and chocolates, and declarations of devotion are a start. But a kindness is better, an act of selflessness which looks for nothing in return. Actions usually speak louder than words.

When Jesus of Nazareth said: 'Love your neighbour as yourself', he wasn't talking about how we might feel about them but about what we might do for them. He told a story about a traveller who stopped at the scene of a mugging, noticed the victim was not from his class or ethnic group and still took time to look after them, get them to hospital and see that they would be cared for. A victim of street violence and a complete stranger. Practical kindness, one human being to another.

Love made real, love as a verb. And a stranger who is seen as a neighbour.

The ancient Hebrew prophets, such as Amos or Hosea, Micah or Isaiah, banged on about how the rich mistreated the poor, about bribery, unpaid labour or political corruption. They knew that love is more than feeling something. That love is doing something.

Loving someone is the most important thing we can do. The early Christian teacher Paul, who on some days was a serious whinge bag, could also find himself taken with moments of transcendent, poetic insight. In one of his most lyrical moments, he compresses all life's virtues down to three: faith, hope … and love, which, he says, is the greatest.

We love someone when we put them at the head of the queue, and ourselves at the back. That's what love does.

And we show love, not to make us look good, but because that's what it's all about.

Love. Actually.

BE ENCHANTED

You …

> Smell the sea.
> Are caught by a familiar song coming from the radio.
> Feel a hand squeeze your shoulder.
> Lie still, looking up, under a great night sky.
> See that person you love approaching.

What you experience, in that moment, is something more than that which your senses capture. An intensity deeper than you expect. A connectedness, a gratitude, a wonder. You feel that this is more real than real.

It might last seconds. Minutes with luck. But it is profound.

Buddhists call feelings like this 'suchness'. Mircea Eliade, a scholar of comparative religions, called them experiences 'of the golden world'. Theologian Marcus Borg talked of being 'filled with glory'.

Everything melts into the present.

In his *Varieties of Religious Experience*, William James recounted an experience of his own when: 'The perfect stillness of the night was thrilled by a more solemn silence. The darkness held a presence that was all the more felt because it was not seen.'

Sometimes we get the sense that there is simply *more*.

This is the 'numinous'.

Experiencing the numinous encourages us to embrace sensations which provide a feeling of being whole, that give us a clue that there may be something beyond.

A moment like this is precious, said William James, and worth holding on to. 'It adds to life an enchantment which is not rationally or logically deducible from anything else …'

BORROWED WISDOM

Greet the day

Eleanor Farjeon, 'Morning Has Broken', Oxford University Press, 1931.

Find the golden hour

Leonardo DiCaprio, interview with Simon Mayo, BBC Radio 5 Live, 5 Jan, 2016. Poem from *Julian of Norwich's Teabag*, by Martin Wroe, Wild Goose Publications, 2022

Record your days

Julia Cameron, *The Artist's Way: A Spiritual Path to Higher Creativity*, Jeremy P. Tarcher, 1992.

Practise kindness

Jane Goodall, 'Being', in the series 'The Secret Lives of Scientists and Engineers', Sept 2014: www.youtube.com/watch?v=0Qu7Wn1mRYA

Dalai Lama, *An Appeal to the World: Ethics Are More Important than Religion*, Benevento, 2016.

Know your place

Amanda Owen, interview with Malcolm Doney, *Church Times*, 22 Dec, 2016.

Thomas Merton, *Conjectures of a Guilty Bystander*, Doubleday, 1966.

Xavier de Maistre, *A Journey around My Room*, 1794.

Live your own life

Bronnie Ware, *The Top Five Regrets of the Dying: A Life Transformed by the Dearly Departing*, Hay House, 2012.

Raymond Carver, 'Gravy', *All of Us: The Collected Poems*, Knopf, 1996.

George Saunders, 'George Saunders' Advice to Graduates', *The New York Times*,

31 Jul 2013, https://6thfloor.blogs.nytimes.com/2013/07/31/george-saunderss-advice-to-graduates

Unplug yourself

Radiohead, *Kid A*, Parlophone, 2000.

John O'Donohue, in conversation with Martin Wroe.

Anne Lamott, '12 Truths I Learned from Life and Writing', Ted Talk, YouTube.

I am because you are

Kurt Vonnegut, *Deadeye Dick*, Delacorte, 1982 (though the phrase had been in circulation since the 1960s).

Brief Meaning of African Word UBUNTU, Ubuntu Women Institute USA, 24 Jan, 2012.

Desmond Tutu, *No Future Without Forgiveness*, Rider & Co., 1999.

Fail again

James Dyson, 'Failure Doesn't Suck', interview with Chuck Salter, *Fast Company* magazine, 5 Jan, 2007.

Neil Gaiman, Commencement Address at the University of the Arts in Philadelphia, 2012.

Samuel Beckett, *Worstward Ho*, Grove, 1983.

Let's take a walk

Stephen and Ondrea Levine, *Who Dies? An Investigation of Conscious Living and Conscious Dying*, Doubleday, 1989.

Douglas Adams, *The Hitchhiker's Guide to the Galaxy*, Pan, 1979.
Herman Melville, *Moby Dick*, 1851.

Ludwig Wittgenstein, 'Journal entry 8 July, 1916', *Notebooks 1914-1916*, Blackwells, 1961.

Take a day off

Thich Nhat Hanh, *The Pocket Thich Nhat Hanh*, Shambhala, 2012.

Ovid, source unknown.

Maya Angelou, *Wouldn't Take Nothing for My Journey Now*, Virago, 1995.

Make big decisions slowly

James Martin, *The Jesuit Guide to Everything*, Harper Collins, 2014.

Anthony Wilson, 'When the Holy Spirit Danced with Me in the Kitchen', *Full Stretch*, Worple Press, 2006.

Pause. Remember. Give thanks. Eat.

Martin Luther King Jr, 'A Christmas Sermon on Peace', in James Melvin Harper (ed.), *A Testament of Hope: The Essential Writings of Martin Luther King Jr*, 1991.

Bart Simpson, 'Two Cars in Every Garage and Three Eyes on Every Fish', *The Simpsons*, Season Two, Episode 7F01, 1 Nov, 1990.

Break bread

Margaret Atwood 'All Bread', *Selected Poems II: Poems Selected and New, 1976-1986*, Oxford University Press, 1986.

What do you plan to do?

Mary Oliver, 'The Summer Day', *New and Selected Poems*, Beacon Press, 1992.

David Brooks, *The Road to Character*, Allen Lane, 2015.

Take the overview

Chris Hedges, 'What Every Person Should Know about War', *The New York Times*, 6 Jul, 2003.

Frank White, *The Overview Effect: Space Exploration and Human Evolution*, Houghton Mifflin, 1987.

Edgar Mitchell, in White, *Overview Effect*.

William Anders, in the film *Overview*.

Live your way into a new kind of thinking

Ann Morisy, *Journeying Out*, Continuum, 2004.

Henri Nouwen, *Life of the Beloved: Spiritual Living in a Secular World*, Crossroad Publishing, 1992.

Light is stronger than darkness

Desmond Tutu, *An African Prayer Book*, Bantam, 1998.

We are not alone

Eugene H. Peterson, *The Message: The Bible in Contemporary Language*, Navpress, 2002.

Play it back

Annie Dillard, *The Writing Life*, Harper and Row, 1989.

Travel light

Søren Kierkegaard, Journals, IV, A 162, 1843.

Paul Ricoeur, *The Symbol of Evil*, Harper Row, 1968.

Ursula K. Le Guin, *The Left Hand of Darkness*, Ace Books. 1969.

Stand still

William Blake, 'Auguries of Innocence', 1863.

Pablo Neruda, 'Keeping Quiet', *Extravagaria*, Jonathan Cape, 1972.

Imagine it

Yuval Noah Harari, *Sapiens: A Brief History of Humankind*, Harvill Secker, 2015.

Fear not

Thich Nhat Hanh, *Fear: Essential Wisdom for Getting Through the Storm*, HarperOne, 2012.

Trust your gut

Bono: *Bono on Bono: Conversations with Michka Assayas*, Hodder & Stoughton, 2006.

Malcolm Gladwell, *Blink: The Power of Thinking Without Thinking*, Little, Brown, 2005.

Interview with Melvyn Bragg, *Third Way* magazine, Jun-Jul, 1996, Vol. 19, no 5.

Tune in

George Herbert, 'Prayer (I)', *The Complete Poetry of George Herbert*, Penguin, 2015.

Anne Lamott, *Plan B: Further Thoughts on Faith*, Riverhead, 2005.

Ann Lewin, 'Disclosure', *Watching for the Kingfisher: Poems and Prayers*, Canterbury Press, 2009.

Like Jesus

Life of Brian, directed by Terry Jones, Handmade Films/Python (Monty) Films, 1979.

The value of nothing

Oscar Wilde, *Lady Windemere's Fan: A Play about a Good Woman*, 1892.

Art Buchwald, source unknown.

Get lost in music

Leonard Bernstein, source unknown.

Douglas Adams, *The Salmon of Doubt*, Heinemann, 2002.

David Bowie, CBS unaired interview, *60 Minutes*, 2003.

Joseph Shabalala, 'A Wise Man Keeps on Singing', interview with David Thomas, *Daily Telegraph*, 27 Jun, 2002.

Mavis Staples, speaking to *Billboard* magazine, 2/20/2020

Remember you are dust

Guy Claxton, *The Wayward Mind: An Intimate History of the Unconscious*, Little, Brown, 2005.

William Wordsworth, 'Tintern Abbey', *Lyrical Ballads, with a Few Other Poems*, Penguin, 2006.

Everybody hurts

Alfred North Whitehead, *Process and Reality*, Free Press, 1978.

Nick Cave, The Red Hand Files #147, www.theredhandfiles.com/utility-of-suffering
REM, 'Everybody Hurts', *Automatic for the People*, Warner Bros, 1992.

Make a habit of it

Anne Lamott, *Bird by Bird: Some Instructions on Writing and Life*, Bantam, 1980.

Karen Armstrong, *The Spiral Staircase*, Anchor, 2004.

Rabbi Chaim Stern, quoted in Rabbi Dennis S. Ross' blog 'On Being', 2 May, 2015, https://onbeing.org/blog/ritual-is-poetry-in-action

Aristotle, quoted in Will Durant, 'Summation of What He Said', *The Story of Philosophy: The Lives and Opinions of the World's Greatest Philosophers*, Simon & Schuster/Pocket Books, 1926.

Don't put a price on it

Lewis Hyde, *The Gift: Imagination and the Erotic Life of Property*, Canongate, 2006.

Join the resistance

Saffiyah Khan, see: https://www.bbc.co.uk/news/av/uk-39555406

Rosa Parks, cited in Donnie Williams and Wayne Greenhaw, *The Thunder of Angels: The Montgomery Bus Boycott and the People Who Broke the Back of Jim Crow*, Chicago Review Press, 2005.

Desmond Tutu, recounted in Walter Wink, *Engaging the Powers*, 25th Anniversary Edition, Fortress Press, 2017.

Duty calls

Albert Camus, *Notebooks 1935-1942*, Knopf, New York, 1963.

Thomas Merton, *No Man Is an Island*, Harcourt, 1978.

God is not a Christian (or Muslim, or Jew, or Buddhist, or Sikh, or Hindu, or agnostic, or atheist …)

Harold S. Kushner, *The Book of Job: When Bad Things Happened to a Good Person*, Schocken Books, 2012.

Richard Rohr, see *Immortal Diamond*, SPCK, 2013, *Falling Upward*, SPCK, 2013.

If in doubt …

Richard Holloway, *Leaving Alexandria: A Memoir of Faith and Doubt*, Canongate, 2012.

John Keats, *The Complete Poetical Works and Letters of John Keats*, Cambridge Edition, Houghton Mifflin & Co., 1889.

Frederick Buechner, see: www.frederickbuechner.com/quote-of-the-day/2016/10/26/doubt

Brené Brown, see: www.citychurchlongbeach.org/dailydevotional/god-is-not-an-epidural-god-is-a-midwife

How and why are different questions

Richard Dawkins, 'Lecture from the Nullifidian', Dec 1994, www.richarddawkins.net

Albert Einstein, 'Letter to Eric Gutkind, 1954', *Letters of Note*, (ed.) Sean Usher Canongate Unbound, 2013.

Jonathan Sacks, *The Great Partnership: God, Science and the Search for Meaning*, Hodder & Stoughton, 2011.

Bear witness

Oliver Sacks, *Awakenings*, Duckworth & Co, 1973.

Elie Wiesel, National Public Radio PR obituary, 2 Jul, 2016, http://www.npr.org/sections/thetwo-way/2016/07/02/166184644/elie-wiesel-holocaust-survivor-and-nobel-laureate-dies-at-87.

Arundhati Roy, *War Talk*, South End Press, 2003.

Reserve your soul

Steven Pinker, *How the Mind Works*, W. W. Norton, 1997.

John O'Donohue, *Anam Cara*, Bantam, 1997.

Find a way home

Walter Brueggemann, *Cadences of Home: Preaching Among Exiles*, Westminster John Knox Press, 2007.

Mahmoud Darwish, interview with Adam Shatz, *The New York Times*, 'A Poet's Palestine as a Metaphor', 22 Dec, 2001.

Expect the unexpected

R.S. Thomas, 'Via Negativa', *Collected Poems 1945-1990*, J.M. Dent, 1993.

George Steiner, *Real Presences*, University of Chicago Press, 1989.

Disorientate yourself

Nick Cave, *The Complete Lyrics 1978-2001*, Penguin, 2001.

Bono, *The Book of Psalms*, Canongate, 1999.

Celebrate religion

REM, 'Losing my Religion', *Out of Time*, Warner Bros, 1991.

Sunday Assembly, www.sundayassembly.com

Linda Woodhead, *Why No Religion Is the New Religion*, British Academy Lecture, 19 Jan, 2016.

Alain de Botton, *Religion for Atheists: A Non-believer's Guide to the Uses of Religion*, Signal, 2012.

Listen to the silence

Blaise Pascal, *Pensées*, 1670 (English translation 1688).

Professor Timothy Wilson, 'Just think: The challenges of the disengaged mind', *Science*, Vol. 345, Issue 6192, 4 Jul, 2014.

Michael Palin, 'Fifty Things to Do in a Church Diocese of London', 16 Aug, 2016, http://www.london.anglican.org/articles/50-things-church

Francis Spufford, *Unapologetic: Why, Despite Everything, Christianity Can Still Make Surprising Emotional Sense*, Faber & Faber, 2012.

This situation shall pass …

Christian Herald and Seaman's Magazine, Volume 8, 1821.

Henri Matisse, *Henri Matisse: The Cut-outs*, Tate Publishing, 2014.

Michael Leunig, *When I Talk to You: A Cartoonist Talks to God*, Andrews McMeel, 2006.

Gaze at the beauty

Hildegard of Bingen, from Matthew Fox, *Original Blessing: A Primer in Creation Spirituality*, Jeremy P Tarcher, 2000.

Thich Nhat Hanh, see:
www.garrisoninstitute.org/blog/insight-of-interbeing

Dorothy Stang, see:
https://rcdow.org.uk/vocations/news/sister-dots-living-legacy

Only remember

Horatius Bonar, 'Only Remembered', 1870.

Own it, note it, fix it

Francis Spufford, *Unapologetic: Why, Despite Everything, Christianity Can Still Make Surprising Emotional Sense*, Faber & Faber, 2012.

Believe in love

Marcus Borg, *Convictions: How I Learned What Matters Most*, Harper One, 2014.

Wait (what?)

Brian Eno, The Long Now Foundation, http://longnow.org

Hear the call

Po Bronson, *What Should I Do with My Life?*, Random House, 2003.

Give thanks

Edna Healey, *The Independent*, Obituary, 23 July, 2010.

W. S. Merwin 'Thanks', *Migration: New and Selected Poems*, Copper Canyon Press, 2005.

Practise resurrection

Wendell Berry, *Manifesto: The Mad Farmer Liberation Front,* Counterpoint, 1973.

Richard Rohr, *The Immortal Diamond: The Search for Our True Self*, Crossroad Publishing Company, 2013.

Love actually

'All You Need Is Love', John Lennon and Paul McCartney, Parlophone, Capitol, 1967.

Be enchanted

Mircea Eliade, *Myth of the Eternal Return: Cosmos and History (Works of Mercea Eliade)*, Princeton University Press, 1971.
Marcus Borg, *Convictions: How I Learned What Matters Most*, HarperOne, 2014.
William James, *Varieties of Religious Experience: A Study in Human Nature*, Longmans Green & Co, 1901.

WHO DO THESE PEOPLE THINK THEY ARE?

Malcolm Doney grew up under the flight path for Heathrow Airport. He studied Fine Art at St Martin's School of Art before pursuing a writing career in journalism, advertising and broadcasting.

He has produced words for factual TV, radio, magazines and newspapers, and written ten books. He is a contributor to BBC Radio 2's *Pause for Thought* and Radio 4's *Something Understood*.

In his mid-fifties, he was ordained as a priest in the Church of England, and volunteers at his parish church in Suffolk. He describes himself as an 'agnostic Christian'.

He has recently returned to art practice, having moved to coastal Suffolk, and had two solo exhibitions in 2022.

He is married to writer and curator, Meryl, and they have two grown-up children.

Martin Wroe is married to Meg, a painter, and together they have been raised by three children.

He got into journalism while studying theology and ended up on the staff of the *Independent* and later the *Observer.* He has had longtime collaborations with the Greenbelt Arts Festival, the human rights NGO Amos Trust and the rock band U2.

He contributes to BBC Radio 4's *Thought for the Day*, is an associate member of the Iona Community and a while back accidentally became an Anglican priest.

He was late to understand that religions are poems and tries to write one most days. His most recent book of poems is *Julian of Norwich's Teabag*.